PHOTOS WITHOUT THE FUSS

HOW TO PRESERVE, ORGANIZE, AND SHARE YOUR PHOTOS FOR SENIORS

VIRGINIA GRANT

INTRODUCTION: WHY ORGANIZING YOUR PHOTOS MATTERS

It's hard to explain exactly why some photographs have the power to stop you in your tracks. One moment, you're scrolling through your phone or opening a folder on your computer, and there it is: a picture from years ago that seems to glow brighter than the others. Perhaps it's a photo of a long-forgotten trip to the beach, the sunlight making everything sparkle, or maybe it's a simple snapshot of a grandchild grinning, frosting all over their cheeks on a birthday morning. Suddenly, you feel it all over again—what it felt like to be there.

That is the gift digital photos can offer when they're easy to find and enjoy. Every picture you've taken holds a little story, even the blurry ones. A story you've lived. And looking back on them can feel like unwrapping those memories all over again.

It doesn't matter if you're just getting used to smartphones or if you've been taking digital pictures for years but haven't quite gotten them organized yet. This part of the process—looking through your memories, one by one—is where everything comes alive. You might even surprise yourself by how much joy it brings.

One woman I spoke with recently shared how much she'd underestimated the simple pleasure of revisiting her old photos. She'd been feeling overwhelmed by the sheer number of pictures she'd collected over the years—thousands of them across her phone, tablet, and computer. But as she started sorting them into folders and deleting the ones she didn't want, she found herself stopping often to really look. There was a picture of her husband leaning on a park bench, waving at the camera with that familiar smirk. Another of her friends standing by a snowman they'd built on a rare snowy day. One evening, she got so caught up looking through her travel photos that she stayed up past midnight laughing to herself.

Those moments are what organizing is really about—not just tidying up files, but giving yourself back a way to connect with your own life.

Even photos you don't think much of when you take them can end up being precious later. A quick shot of a kitchen table might bring back a memory of holiday mornings with kids tearing into wrapping paper. A picture of an ordinary street corner can remind you of the time you and your neighbor stopped there to chat about the weather. Small things you thought you'd forget suddenly feel vivid again.

Digital photos also let you relive memories you weren't even there for. A niece might send a picture of her baby's first steps. A friend might share a snapshot of a dinner party you couldn't attend. These are glimpses into moments you'd otherwise miss, and being able to save them—and find them again later—makes them feel just as much a part of your story.

There's something comforting about knowing your life is right there in front of you, too. When you've been through hard times, looking back at pictures can remind you how much you've already lived through. A photo of yourself smiling on a vacation years ago can be a quiet kind of encouragement. You've been happy before; you'll be happy again.

And, of course, there are the people we miss. Photos can bring them closer in a way words can't quite manage. A picture of someone you loved who's no longer here might bring tears to your eyes, but it can also bring a smile. Being able to see their face, their hands, even the way they stood, can feel like a small reunion every time you click on that file.

That's why taking time with your pictures is worth it. They aren't just files on a screen or icons in a folder. They're little pieces of you. Little moments you've lived, ready to meet you again whenever you need them.

Why digital photos tend to get "lost"

It doesn't take long for a collection of digital photos to feel like a maze. You might sit down at your computer, open your phone, or even plug in a camera card and scroll through hundreds—sometimes thousands—of little rectangles, each one representing a moment you've lived. And yet, when you're looking for that one special picture, it can feel as though it's vanished into thin air.

This happens more often than most people expect. One of the great blessings of digital photography is that you can take as many pictures as you like without worrying about running out of film. That freedom, however, comes at a cost: sheer volume. A few snapshots here and there turn into dozens, then hundreds, then thousands, and before long, it feels like you're buried under them.

Part of the challenge is that digital photos don't take up physical space you can see. In the days of printed pictures, you might have a shoebox under the bed or albums lined up on a shelf. They were right where you left them, and even if they weren't neatly labeled, you at least knew where to start looking. Digital photos, on the other hand, are stored as files on devices—sometimes several devices—and they don't always show up where you expect them.

Each phone, computer, and camera organizes pictures slightly differently. Phones save them in the camera roll, but that same photo might also be sent to a cloud service without you realizing it. Cameras save images on little memory cards that can be tucked into a drawer and forgotten. If you email or text a picture to someone and later want to save it yourself, it might stay hidden in an inbox or messaging app. It's no wonder people sometimes feel like their pictures disappear.

Even the names of the files make it harder to keep track of things. Digital photos are usually named by the device that took them: something like DSC_0123.jpg or IMG_4567. It's not exactly helpful when you're trying to find the shot of your granddaughter's school play or that trip you took to the mountains. Every file looks the same until you open it. And opening hundreds one at a time is no way to spend an afternoon.

Technology can also work against you in subtle ways. Many devices automatically create backups in the cloud—helpful in theory—but they often make duplicates or store things in odd places. A single picture might live on your phone, in your email, and in the cloud all at once, each copy with a different date or resolution. Then there are the photos that don't get backed up at all, staying trapped on an old phone or forgotten computer.

Over time, most people simply give up trying to keep it all straight. Photos just pile up in whatever order they were taken, and even finding a picture from last Christmas becomes a frustrating task. Worse, some images get deleted by mistake, or lost when a device fails.

It's worth noting that digital photos also get "lost" in a

more emotional sense. When they're buried in disorganized folders or hidden behind hundreds of random shots, you stop looking at them altogether. The moments you once wanted to remember most become just another file buried on a hard drive, unseen and unappreciated.

There's also the fact that the more photos you have, the harder it feels to start sorting them. The idea of tackling a mountain of images can feel overwhelming—where to begin? That feeling keeps many people from even trying, letting the collection grow larger and more chaotic. Before you know it, years have passed, and you can't even remember which device holds what.

The good news is that once you understand why it happens, you can begin to take control. None of this is your fault—it's simply the way digital photography has developed. Manufacturers and software designers rarely think about what it feels like for someone trying to keep track of thousands of precious memories. But you can change that.

How organizing helps you find and share your best moments

The feeling of clicking through endless screens of photos just to find one favorite memory can be exhausting. Every swipe or scroll takes you past dozens of similar shots, blurry pictures, and duplicates, and yet the one you really want remains buried somewhere you can't quite reach. It's no wonder people give up and settle for whatever's easiest to grab. But when you take the time to organize your collection, those frustrations start to fade. You begin to see your memories as they're meant to be seen—clearly, and without a struggle.

Organizing your photos is not about creating rules or forcing yourself into a rigid system. It's about giving your memories a home where they can be found and appreciated when you need them. It's about turning a pile of digital clutter into something you can actually enjoy.

One of the first benefits you'll notice after organizing is how quickly you can find the moments that matter most. A birthday party from five years ago, a sunset from a family trip, a favorite picture of your grandchildren—suddenly, these aren't hidden in a sea of file names and random dates. They're right there, ready to bring a smile to your face.

This becomes even more meaningful when someone else asks for a photo. Perhaps a friend wants to see a picture from a vacation you took together. Or your granddaughter asks if you have any baby pictures she can show at school. Instead of shrugging or spending twenty minutes searching, you can open your albums, click once or twice, and send it off within seconds. That ease not only saves time, but it also makes sharing your life with others feel natural again.

Sharing photos has a way of deepening connections. When you can easily pull up the right picture and send it to someone you love, you're sending more than an image. You're saying, "This mattered to me, and I want you to have it too." Whether it's by email, text, or even printed and mailed, these small gestures can brighten someone's day and keep your relationships strong.

Organizing also helps you discover patterns you may not have noticed before. As you sort your photos into folders or albums, you'll start seeing the chapters of your life in a new way. You might notice how often you've photographed gardens, or how each Christmas morning looks a little different as children grow. You may find a whole series of quiet moments you forgot you'd even captured—little signs of what's important to you.

There's something very comforting about having your photos tell your story in a way you can actually follow. Instead of a jumble of random shots, you see your life in seasons, in milestones, in favorite faces and familiar places. Those connections can be powerful.

Even photos you thought you didn't care much about take on new meaning when they're easy to find. A picture of your street after a snowstorm, a neighbor dropping by for coffee, a quiet morning in the park—these small, ordinary moments become treasures when they're not lost among hundreds of unrelated files.

Another benefit is peace of mind. Once your photos are organized, you're no longer worried about whether you'll be able to find something if you ever need it. You don't have to fear that a special memory has been lost forever just because it's sitting somewhere you can't remember. That kind of relief is worth the effort all by itself.

And when it comes to backing up your collection, having everything in order makes the process much easier. Instead of trying to back up a confusing mess of folders and random files, you can copy entire albums or neatly labeled folders to the cloud or an external drive. That keeps your memories safe while also keeping your mind at ease.

People sometimes think organizing photos means they have to get everything perfect, but perfection isn't the goal. You don't have to name every single file or sort every single image in a single sitting. Even small steps—like putting your favorite events into separate folders or deleting a few blurry duplicates—can make a noticeable difference.

Little by little, you'll start to see the results. The next time someone asks for a copy of that funny picture from last Thanksgiving, you'll know exactly where it is. The next time you feel like revisiting your trip to Italy, you can open a folder full of just those memories, ready to enjoy.

One of the most rewarding moments happens when you share your organized collection with others. Sitting down with family and showing them an album you've created can spark laughter, stories, and even a few happy tears. Sending an old photo to a friend you haven't seen in years can reconnect you in ways you didn't expect. These are the kinds of conversations and memories that organizing makes possible.

Reassurance: You don't need to be a computer whiz

It's natural to feel a little intimidated by technology at first, especially when the words, buttons, and screens seem to change every time you look. Many people believe that only someone "good with computers" can manage digital photos, but the truth is much simpler than that. You don't need to know everything about devices, software, or settings to get your memories organized and easy to enjoy.

What you really need is patience and a willingness to take one step at a time. That's all. The rest comes with practice.

You may have heard younger relatives toss around phrases like "file format" or "cloud sync" and felt left out of the conversation. That can make anyone feel as though they're not keeping up. But those are just fancy words for simple ideas, and none of them are beyond your reach. Much of the confusion comes from the way technology companies design their products. They don't always explain things in plain language, which makes it feel more complicated than it is.

The good news is that every device, whether it's a phone, tablet, or computer, was designed to be used by people just like you. They were made to make life easier, not harder. If you can learn to turn it on, open your photos, and tap or click a few buttons, you already have everything you need to get started. You don't have to memorize long instructions or understand every option on the screen.

One of the biggest misconceptions people carry is the idea that they need to be "fast" or "fluent" with computers to succeed. There's no race to win here. There's no quiz to pass. You can take all the time you want to look through your photos, try different steps, and even make mistakes. Mistakes aren't disasters; they're how you learn.

Even those who've used computers for decades still make errors and forget how to do things. The difference is, they've learned not to panic when that happens. A wrong tap or click usually isn't permanent. If something doesn't look right, you can always close it and try again. And if you truly can't figure something out, help is never far away.

Another worry people often have is that their hands might not be quick or steady enough to use a touchscreen, or their eyes might not catch all the little details on a screen. That's perfectly understandable. The technology was not designed with everyone's hands or eyes in mind, but there are simple adjustments you can make to suit yourself. You can make the text bigger, adjust the brightness of the screen, or even buy a stylus—a little pen-shaped tool that can make touching the screen easier. None of these fixes require you to be an expert.

One of the most powerful habits you can develop is asking questions. Whether you're asking a friend, family member, or even searching for an answer online, there's no shame in needing help. Everyone does. Even professionals rely on guides and instructions. And once you learn something once, it's yours to keep.

It can also help to remember how much you've already learned in life. You've probably used a microwave, driven a car, and maybe even programmed a VCR back when those were popular. At one point, every single one of those skills was new and unfamiliar. But you figured them out, one button at a time. This is no different.

Don't let labels like "tech-savvy" or "digital native" convince you that technology belongs to someone else. You have every right to use these tools to your advantage. And you don't need to know every single feature of your device to use it well. Most people only ever use a small portion of what their devices can do, and that's just fine.

In fact, one of the smartest things you can do is ignore anything that feels unnecessary. Many apps and programs are filled with extra features you'll never need. Stick to the basics: viewing your photos, moving them into folders or albums, deleting the ones you don't want, and backing up the ones you love. Those four actions are enough to bring order to even the most cluttered collection.

1

UNDERSTANDING THE BASICS OF DIGITAL PHOTOS

At first glance, a digital photo seems simple. You take a picture on your phone, your camera, or even a tablet, and there it is on the screen—a moment captured, ready to view and share. But behind that familiar image is something a little more technical. A digital photo isn't a single solid thing like a printed picture; it's a file. And every file has its own type, which explains how it's saved, how much space it takes up, and where it can be opened or shared.

Understanding what a digital photo actually is can help you feel more in control when you start organizing and working with your collection. You don't have to become an expert, and you don't need to know every detail of how it works. What you do need is a basic sense of what these file types mean, why they exist, and when you might want to pay attention to them.

At its most basic level, a digital photo is made up of tiny pieces of information called pixels. Each pixel is like a single dot of color, and together they make up the full image. When you take a picture, your device records all those dots and saves them as a file, storing all the necessary information about colors, shapes, and light.

Where things get slightly more complicated is in how that file is saved. There are different ways to store a digital image, and these are known as file formats. Each one has its own strengths, weaknesses, and best uses. The good news is that most of the time you don't need to choose the format yourself—your device does it for you. But when you start organizing, sharing, or printing your pictures, it can be helpful to know what those letters—JPG, PNG, HEIC—mean.

The most common file type you'll see is **JPG**. Sometimes it's written as **JPEG**, but the two are the same. This format has been around for decades, and it's the standard for most cameras and phones. JPG files are popular because they keep the photo's quality high enough to look good while keeping the file size small enough to store and send easily. They're widely supported, meaning they can be opened on just about any device or program without trouble. If you see a photo ending in .jpg or .jpeg, you can feel confident it will work just about anywhere.

One reason JPG is so common is that it "compresses" the photo. That means it removes tiny bits of information you're unlikely to notice in order to shrink the file size. For everyday use—sharing online, printing regular photos, emailing pictures to family—this works perfectly. There is a trade-off, though. Because JPG files lose some of the original data when they're saved, they're not ideal if you plan to do heavy editing or blow the picture up to a large poster size.

Another file type you might encounter is **PNG**. This one is less common for casual photography but is often used for graphics, designs, or photos where transparency is needed. A PNG file doesn't compress as much as a JPG, which means it can hold more detail and doesn't lose quality every time it's saved. It's especially good for things like screenshots or simple images with sharp edges and text. The trade-off is that PNG files tend to be much larger, which makes them harder to store in large numbers.

More recently, newer devices, particularly iPhones and iPads, have started using a format called **HEIC**, which stands for High Efficiency Image Coding. Apple introduced this to save space on your device because HEIC files are much smaller than JPGs while keeping the photo quality very high. This is why you might notice your iPhone seems to store thousands of photos without running out of space too quickly.

The downside of HEIC is that it's not yet as universally supported as JPG. Some older computers or programs might not open HEIC files without converting them first. Luckily, Apple devices handle this automatically in many cases, and you can even adjust your settings to save in JPG instead if you prefer.

You may also come across **GIFs**, which are more commonly used for short animations or moving images rather than regular photos. GIF files aren't ideal for preserving high-quality photographs because they're limited in the number of colors they can display. They're fun for sharing little animations, but not something you'll need for organizing family memories.

Occasionally, someone with a more advanced camera may use formats like **RAW** or **TIFF**. These file types hold all the information from the camera sensor without compression, which makes them much larger in size but also more flexible for professional editing. For most everyday photography, you won't have to worry about RAW or TIFF files, but you may see them mentioned if you've worked with a photographer or tried printing large professional prints.

Each of these file types has its place, but there's no need to feel overwhelmed. For most people, the majority of their digital photos will already be in JPG or HEIC format. And both of these work beautifully for organizing, sharing, and printing memories.

When you start organizing your pictures, you may notice your collection includes a mix of file types. This happens because devices and apps often save photos in slightly different ways. Your phone may save in HEIC, while your email attachments come through as JPGs, and a downloaded image from the internet might be a PNG. That's perfectly normal and nothing to worry about.

Where your photos live

When you take a photo, it's easy to forget what actually happens to it afterward. The picture appears on your screen, you smile at it, and then you move on. But behind the scenes, that moment has to find somewhere to live—a place to stay until you're ready to look at it again, share it, or print it. Understanding where your photos live is an important part of keeping them organized and easy to find.

One of the biggest reasons people feel overwhelmed by their digital photo collections is that pictures often scatter themselves across different devices and services. A few are saved on your phone, some are stuck on a camera memory card, others are hiding in old computer folders, and then there's the cloud quietly storing even more. This scattering can feel confusing, but it doesn't have to.

Start with the place most people think of first: your **phone.** For many, the phone is the main camera these days. Every time you tap the shutter, the photo gets saved directly into the phone's internal storage. On most phones, there's a built-in app that organizes these pictures for you. It might be called "Photos," "Gallery," or "Camera Roll," and it shows all the pictures you've taken, usually in chronological order.

Phones have limited space, though. Every picture you take uses a little bit of that storage, and over time, your phone can fill up. Many phones now automatically upload photos to a cloud service in the background to free up space. That's why you might notice photos disappearing from your phone but still being viewable through the Photos app—what you're actually seeing may be stored elsewhere.

Next is your **camera**, if you use one. Many people still enjoy using a separate digital camera for vacations or special events. These cameras save pictures onto a memory card, also called an SD card. The card acts as the camera's storage, holding your pictures until you move them somewhere else. Unlike a phone, the camera itself isn't where you keep your pictures long term. At some point, you'll need to transfer those images to another device—a computer, a tablet, or even directly to a cloud service—because the card will eventually run out of room.

Then there's your **computer**. For years, the computer was the natural home for digital photos. You'd plug in your camera or phone, transfer your pictures, and store them in folders right there on your hard drive. Even today, the computer remains a great central place for your collection because it offers more storage than a phone and gives you more control over how to organize your pictures. On a computer, you can create folders named by date, event, or person, and you can back them up onto an external drive or cloud service later.

Sometimes, people forget just how many photos are already sitting on their computer's hard drive. Between downloads, email attachments, and transfers from cameras over the years, computers often hold treasures you've forgotten about. It can be worth taking the time to explore what's already there before adding more.

And then there's the **cloud**, which may feel like the most mysterious of all. The cloud is really just a term for storage on someone else's servers, which you access through the internet. Services like Apple iCloud, Google Photos, Amazon Photos, and Dropbox all offer to store your pictures in the cloud, freeing up space on your phone or computer.

When you use the cloud, your pictures don't physically live on your device anymore—or at least not entirely. Instead, you can open an app or website and see your entire library from any device connected to the internet. This is incredibly handy because it keeps your collection accessible even if you lose or replace your phone or computer.

The cloud does come with its own quirks. If you're not careful, you might end up with duplicates if you're also storing copies on your computer and phone. Or you may get confused about which version is the most recent. Some cloud services only save smaller versions of your pictures unless you pay for more storage. It's worth learning the basics of how your cloud service works, so you know what's being stored and where.

It's also possible for your photos to live in more than one place at once. For example, you might take a photo with your phone, which saves it to your camera roll. That phone may also back it up automatically to iCloud or Google Photos. Later, you might transfer a copy of it to your computer for safekeeping. And if you email it to a friend, that picture also lives in your email account.

This overlapping can feel a little chaotic, but it also means you're less likely to lose something completely. Once you start organizing, you'll learn how to keep track of where your main copies are and how to clean up the extras if you want to free up space.

One of the most helpful steps you can take is to pick one place to be the "home" for your collection. That doesn't mean you can't use the cloud or your phone, but having a central location—often your computer or a cloud account—makes it much easier to keep track of everything. You can still keep smaller copies on your devices to view and share as you like.

How many photos most people have — and why it feels overwhelming

It can come as a shock to open your photo app or computer folder one day and see the number at the bottom of the screen: thousands and thousands of pictures staring back at you. Even people who don't think of themselves as heavy photo-takers are often surprised by just how many images they've collected over the years. And that surprise often comes with a sinking feeling—how can anyone possibly sort through all of it?

You're not alone in that reaction. The average person today has far more digital photos than they realize. On a typical smartphone, it's common to find anywhere from 5,000 to 10,000 pictures saved. Many people have even more if they've been using the same device for years or if they regularly transfer their pictures from old phones without deleting duplicates. Add in folders on computers, pictures saved from emails, social media downloads, and memory cards from cameras, and that number can double or triple without much effort.

Part of the reason the number grows so quickly is that taking a digital photo is so easy—and free. In the days of film cameras, every click of the shutter cost something. You had to buy film, have it developed, and wait to see the results. People thought more carefully about what was worth photographing. But once digital cameras became standard, and especially once smartphones put cameras in everyone's pocket, that barrier disappeared. Now you can take dozens of pictures of the same scene, just to make sure you get one you like. And since there's no cost or waiting involved, most people never bother to delete the extras.

That's one reason digital photo collections feel so overwhelming: they're filled with things you didn't really mean to keep. There are blurry shots, duplicates, accidental screenshots, and pictures of random receipts or grocery lists you took just to remember something for a moment. Mixed in with those are the precious memories you do care about—birthdays, vacations, family gatherings—but they're surrounded by noise. That noise is what makes the task of organizing feel bigger than it really is.

Another reason the numbers creep up is automatic saving. Many phones and apps now save every single picture you take, whether you meant to keep it or not. On top of that, cloud services like iCloud or Google Photos often save multiple copies of the same photo from different devices. If you've ever wondered why your photo count seems much higher than what you remember taking, this is probably part of the reason. Your pictures may be duplicated across your phone, your computer, and the cloud.

It also feels overwhelming because most of us don't look at our collections regularly. The photos simply pile up in the background, quietly increasing day by day. It's like a closet you never clean out—every time you open it, there's more and more stuffed inside, and the idea of tackling it becomes less appealing. The longer you wait, the bigger the job seems.

On top of the sheer number of photos, there's often an emotional weight to the task. Each image represents a moment, and looking at them all at once can bring up a mix of feelings—happiness, nostalgia, even sadness or regret. That emotional layer makes it harder to approach the task of organizing with a clear head. It's easy to feel paralyzed, unsure where to start, and afraid you'll make a mistake by deleting something important.

There's also the problem of decision fatigue. Every single photo you look at asks you to make a choice: keep or delete? Move it or leave it? Which folder does it belong in? When you're looking at hundreds or thousands of photos in a row, those little decisions can feel exhausting. This is a normal response, and it doesn't mean you're doing anything wrong—it just means you need a way to approach it that feels manageable.

Even the variety of devices and storage locations can add to the sense of chaos. You might have some pictures on your phone, some on an old tablet, some on your computer, and some saved in the cloud. Each of those places might have its own set of duplicates and disorganized folders. It can feel like you're chasing your memories through a maze, never sure where they'll turn up next.

What's important to keep in mind is that none of this is your fault. The way technology works now practically invites this kind of clutter. Companies have made it easy to take and store photos, but they haven't made it easy to organize them. Most people end up with an overwhelming collection because they're doing exactly what the devices were designed to encourage: taking lots of pictures and letting the device save them automatically.

Once you understand how the clutter happens, though, it becomes easier to see a path forward. You don't have to tackle everything at once, and you don't have to achieve perfection. Even small steps, taken a little at a time, can make a big difference.

One of the first steps is simply acknowledging how many pictures you have and where they're stored. Checking the number in your phone's gallery or your computer's photos folder gives you a starting point. Knowing where your pictures are—on your phone, your camera's memory card, your computer, or the cloud—lets you begin to think about how you want to bring them all together in one place.

Knowing what you want: keep, delete, share

When you're staring at hundreds—or even thousands—of digital pictures, one of the biggest challenges isn't where to find them. It's deciding what to actually *do* with them. Every picture on your screen represents a choice, and that can feel heavier than expected. But learning to sort through your photos with intention—figuring out what you want to keep, what you're willing to delete, and what you'd love to share—makes the process feel lighter and much more manageable.

This is about more than just cleaning up clutter. It's about clarifying what matters to you, what memories bring you joy, and what stories you want to tell. And the truth is, you already know these things. The goal here is simply to connect that knowledge to the decisions you make while organizing your pictures.

The first step is deciding what you truly want to **keep**. It's tempting to think you have to keep everything just in case you want it later. But when you hold onto every single image, it becomes harder to see the ones that mean the most to you. Take your time and look at each picture, even if just for a moment. Ask yourself: does this photo make me feel something good? Does it show a memory I want to revisit? Does it help tell the story of my life or the lives of people I care about? If the answer is yes, keep it.

What you choose to keep will be different from what someone else might keep, and that's perfectly fine. Your choices are personal. Some people like to save every picture of a grandchild, even if some are blurry or awkward. Others only keep the best one from a set. Some save pictures of scenery from trips, while others prefer to focus on family and friends. The point is not to meet someone else's standard, but your own.

It also helps to remember that keeping a picture doesn't mean you're keeping just the image—it means you're keeping the story behind it. If a blurry shot still makes you smile because of who was there or what was happening, it's worth keeping. But if a photo doesn't stir anything in you, or it's just another version of one you've already decided to keep, you can let it go.

That brings us to what to **delete**. For many people, deleting photos feels risky at first. You might worry about regretting it later, or feel like you're throwing away a memory. But deleting isn't about erasing your past—it's about clearing away the distractions so you can better see what really matters.

There are certain types of photos you can delete without much thought: duplicates, accidental screenshots, pictures that are too blurry to recognize, and random shots you took of receipts, menus, or products in a store. These clutter up your collection without adding any real value.

Then there are the harder decisions—pictures of events you didn't enjoy, people you no longer speak to, or moments that bring more pain than joy. Some people choose to keep these as part of their life's story. Others feel lighter when they let them go. Only you can decide which is right for you.

It can be helpful to think of your photo collection as a garden. Every garden has weeds that need pulling and branches that need pruning, not because they're bad, but because they're taking up space and blocking the view of the flowers. Deleting unnecessary photos is just another way of tending to your memories and making room for the ones that truly matter.

Then comes the part many people find the most rewarding: deciding what to **share**. Digital photos are meant to be seen and enjoyed, and sharing them is one of the best ways to reconnect with others. Once you've sorted through your collection and found your favorites, you can pick out the ones that you want to send to friends or family, post on social media, or even print and give as gifts.

Sharing photos helps you tell the stories you want others to know. It lets you say, "This moment meant something to me, and I want you to see it." Sometimes it's a group shot from a family reunion, other times it's a quiet sunset you watched alone but thought someone else might appreciate. Sharing strengthens connections and reminds you that your memories are part of something larger than yourself.

It's worth thinking about how you'd like to share as well. You might send individual pictures through text or email, create a digital album to share with family, or print a small photo book as a gift. You don't have to decide all at once, and you don't have to share everything with everyone. Sometimes the most meaningful pictures are the ones you share with just one other person at the right moment.

Making decisions about which photos to keep, delete, and share takes practice, and it's normal to feel unsure at first. Give yourself permission to go slowly. Work in short sessions rather than trying to do it all at once. Some people find it helpful to make three folders—one for keeps, one for deletions, and one for sharing—and move photos into those as they go. This keeps the process simple and avoids second-guessing yourself.

It also helps to remind yourself that none of these decisions are final. If you keep something now but decide later that you don't need it, you can always delete it then. And if you delete something by mistake, many devices and cloud services have a "recently deleted" folder where you can recover it.

2

GETTING TO KNOW YOUR DEVICES

Using your smartphone

For most people today, the smartphone has become the main way to capture, view, and share photos. Whether you carry an iPhone, an Android, or even an older model, your phone is likely packed with features that make managing your pictures much easier than you might think. Understanding the basics of how to use your smartphone for your photos not only saves time but also takes away much of the stress that can come from staring at a screen full of icons and buttons you're not sure about.

One of the first things to know is that every smartphone comes with a built-in camera app. On an iPhone, it's simply called "Camera." On most Android phones, it may be called "Camera," "Samsung Camera," or "Google Camera," depending on the brand. You don't need to download anything extra—just tap the icon that looks like a little camera and you're ready to take pictures.

When you open the camera, you'll see the view from the lens on your screen. There's a large circle near the bottom that acts as the shutter button. A single tap takes a photo. Holding it down usually starts a short video. On both iPhones and Android phones, you can also swipe the screen to switch between different modes like Video, Portrait, or Panorama. These extra modes can be fun to explore, but you don't need to use them to take regular pictures.

After you take a picture, your phone automatically saves it to its internal memory and places it in your photo gallery. On an iPhone, this app is called "Photos." On Android phones, it might be called "Gallery" or "Google Photos." When you open that app, you'll see all your pictures arranged by date, with the most recent ones at the bottom or top depending on your settings.

One helpful thing about using a smartphone is that it organizes photos for you without any extra work on your part. Both iPhones and Androids group your pictures by date, and they even try to sort them into collections like "Trips" or "People." You don't have to use those features if you don't want to, but it's nice to know they're there.

You can also favorite photos to find them more easily later. On an iPhone, open a picture and tap the little heart icon. On Android, you might see a star or an option to "Add to favorites" in the menu. This is useful when you're sorting through pictures and see ones you know you'll want to find quickly.

Deleting photos is just as easy. When you're viewing a picture you don't want to keep, look for the trash can icon and tap it. Don't worry too much about deleting something by accident—both iPhones and Androids send deleted pictures to a "Recently Deleted" or "Trash" folder for several weeks before they're permanently erased. You can always go there to recover a picture if you change your mind.

Sharing pictures from your smartphone is straightforward too. Open the photo you'd like to share and look for the square icon with an arrow pointing up (on iPhone) or the three dots or "Share" icon (on Android). This brings up a menu with options to send your picture through email, text message, or even directly to social media apps like Facebook or Instagram if you use them.

One of the most common questions people have is about storage. Both iPhones and Android phones only have so much room to hold your pictures. If you take lots of photos, you may eventually see a message saying you're running low on space. When that happens, it usually means it's time to back up your pictures to the cloud or transfer them to another device, like a computer or external drive, to free up room.

Both types of smartphones also offer cloud backup options. On an iPhone, you can turn on iCloud Photos in your settings. This automatically uploads your pictures to your iCloud account and lets you see them on other Apple devices or by logging in online. On Android, you can use Google Photos for a similar effect. Once turned on, Google Photos keeps a copy of all your pictures safely stored online.

Another basic feature worth knowing about is how to search through your pictures. In the Photos app (on iPhone) and Google Photos app (on Android), there's a search bar you can use to type in things like "beach," "dog," or even the name of a person if your phone has learned who they are. This is incredibly helpful when you're looking for a specific memory in a large collection.

Smartphones are also designed to help you edit your photos right after you take them. Open a picture and look for the "Edit" button. You'll see options to crop the photo, adjust brightness and color, or even apply filters to change the mood of the picture. You don't have to use these tools, but they can make a good photo look even better without much effort.

If you use a smartphone with a touch screen, you might already be comfortable with pinching to zoom in and swiping left or right to move through your pictures. These simple gestures make browsing your collection feel natural and intuitive, even if you've never thought much about it before.

It's also worth mentioning that smartphones can connect directly to printers or photo kiosks in many stores now. If you'd like to print a picture, you can often send it wirelessly to a printer at home or plug your phone into a kiosk at a store like Walgreens or CVS. Many of these kiosks walk you through the process step by step right on the screen.

One of the nicest things about using your smartphone for photos is that it keeps everything in one place. You don't have to fumble with memory cards or wonder which folder on your computer holds the picture you're looking for. You can open your photo app and scroll through your memories right in your hand.

Using a digital camera and transferring pictures

Even in a world full of smartphones, there's still something special about using a digital camera. Many people find that a dedicated camera offers a sense of focus and purpose that a phone doesn't. It feels intentional—like you're truly taking the time to capture a memory. Digital cameras also have some advantages, like better zoom, higher-quality lenses, and more control over lighting and focus. Whether you already own one or are thinking of picking it up again, understanding how to use a digital camera alongside your other devices can be surprisingly simple.

Most modern digital cameras work in much the same way. You press the power button, look through the viewfinder or at the back screen, frame your shot, and press the shutter button to capture the image. The camera saves each picture to a memory card, often called an SD card. This little card is the key to everything—it's where all your photos live until you transfer them to another device.

Many cameras have options to change how your pictures are captured. You might see menus with terms like "Auto," "Portrait," "Night," or "Sports." These settings adjust the camera for different situations. If you prefer to keep things simple, leaving the camera on Auto is perfectly fine. It will adjust itself to give you a good photo without you needing to think about the technical details.

When you're ready to look at your pictures, most cameras let you review them on the back screen. You can scroll through, zoom in to check the details, and even delete bad shots right there if you want. But for organizing and preserving your memories, you'll eventually need to transfer your photos off the camera and onto something more permanent—like a computer, an external drive, or the cloud.

Transferring your photos is one of the most important parts of using a digital camera, and it's easier than it might seem. There are a few common ways to do it, and you can choose the one that feels most comfortable.

The most direct method is to remove the memory card from the camera. To do this, turn the camera off, find the little slot where the card lives (usually on the side or bottom of the camera), and gently push the card in until it pops out. Then insert the card into your computer's card reader slot, if it has one. Most laptops and desktops have a slot for SD cards. If yours doesn't, you can buy an inexpensive card reader that plugs into your computer's USB port.

Once the card is connected to your computer, you'll see it appear as a folder or drive. You can then open it, view your pictures, and drag them into a folder on your computer. Many people like to create a folder with the date or event name—something like "Family Reunion July 2022"—to keep things organized. After you've transferred the pictures, you can choose whether to delete them from the card to free up space for your next adventure.

Another way to transfer photos is by connecting the camera itself directly to your computer using a USB cable. Most cameras come with a cable in the box. Plug one end into the camera and the other into your computer. Turn the camera on, and your computer should recognize it automatically. You can then open the camera just like a folder and copy the pictures to your computer. This method is handy if you prefer not to fuss with removing and reinserting the memory card.

Some newer cameras even have wireless options. If your camera supports Wi-Fi or Bluetooth, you can connect it to your home network or your phone and transfer pictures wirelessly. The exact steps vary by camera model, but many manufacturers have free apps you can download to guide you through the process. This is convenient if you prefer to skip cables altogether.

Once your pictures are safely transferred, it's wise to back them up. Copy them to an external hard drive or upload them to a cloud service. This way, even if your computer has a problem or your memory card gets lost, your memories are still safe.

One thing to keep in mind about digital cameras is that they often save higher-quality files than phones. That's great for printing large photos or preserving every little detail, but it also means the files are bigger and take up more space. If you use a digital camera often, you might want to invest in extra memory cards or a larger external drive for storage.

Using a digital camera alongside your smartphone gives you the best of both worlds. Your phone is always with you, ready for quick snapshots. Your camera, on the other hand, is there for the moments you want to capture in more detail. Many people find that having both lets them enjoy photography more, without feeling tied to just one way of doing things.

One of the benefits of getting comfortable with transferring photos is that it helps you stay organized. Instead of letting your memory cards pile up with thousands of pictures, you can regularly move your images to your computer, delete the ones you don't want, and start fresh with an empty card. This keeps your camera ready for the next time you need it and ensures your photos are stored safely in one place.

Using a tablet or computer

Tablets and computers play an important role in organizing, viewing, and enjoying your photos. While smartphones and cameras are excellent for capturing moments, they're not always the best tools for managing a collection. A larger screen, a keyboard and mouse, and more storage make tablets and computers particularly useful when you want to take control of your digital memories. Understanding how to use them effectively can turn what feels like a daunting task into something far more approachable.

A tablet, like an iPad or a Samsung Galaxy Tab, is essentially a big smartphone without the phone calls. It's light, portable, and easy to use with just your fingers. The larger screen makes it more comfortable for browsing through photos and editing them. If you already use a smartphone, learning to use a tablet feels very familiar, as many of the icons, menus, and apps are the same.

On a tablet, your pictures are typically stored in an app called "Photos" or "Gallery." If you already back up your pictures to the cloud—through iCloud, Google Photos, or another service—your tablet can access all those same images automatically. This is one of the biggest advantages of a tablet: you can see your entire collection without worrying about transferring files from your phone or camera. Just connect the tablet to your home Wi-Fi, open the photo app, and start scrolling.

Tablets also let you edit photos more comfortably. The larger screen helps you see small details you might miss on a phone. You can crop, adjust colors, remove red-eye, or add filters with just a few taps. Many tablets also support a stylus or pen if you prefer more precision. Even small tasks, like adding captions or organizing into albums, feel easier when you're not squinting at a tiny phone screen.

Sharing photos from a tablet is just as simple. Whether you want to email a photo, post it on social media, or show it on a bigger screen, a tablet gives you more room to work and see what you're doing. If you like to create digital photo books or slideshows, tablets also support a wide variety of apps that guide you through the process step by step.

Moving to a computer gives you even more power and flexibility. While tablets are great for convenience, computers are unmatched when it comes to storage, organization, and creating backups. Whether you use a desktop or a laptop, your computer can become the central hub for your entire photo collection.

On a computer, your pictures are typically stored in a folder system that you can control entirely. You can create folders by year, event, person, or place—whatever makes the most sense to you. This kind of structure makes it much easier to find what you're looking for later.

When you transfer pictures from your camera, phone, or memory card to your computer, you can decide exactly where they go. Many people find it helpful to create one main folder called "Pictures" or "Photos," and then add subfolders within it. For example, inside "Pictures," you might have folders named "2021," "2022," and "2023," with each year containing folders for birthdays, vacations, holidays, and other events.

Computers also have more storage than phones or tablets. You don't have to worry about filling up space as quickly, especially if you also have an external hard drive. This makes a computer the ideal place to store your master copies while leaving smaller versions on your portable devices.

On both Windows and Mac computers, you can use built-in apps to view and organize your photos. Windows has the "Photos" app, which automatically organizes your pictures by date and lets you create albums, slideshows, and even quick edits. Macs have the "Photos" app as well, which syncs with iCloud if you use Apple devices. Both systems are designed to be user-friendly, but they also let you dig deeper if you like having full control.

One of the biggest benefits of using a computer is how much easier it is to back up your collection. You can copy your entire photo library to an external drive in just a few minutes. You can also connect your computer to cloud services like Google Drive, Dropbox, or iCloud to keep an online backup of your pictures.

Computers also make it possible to work with specialized software if you want to go beyond the basics. Programs like

Adobe Lightroom, Photoshop Elements, or other photo managers let you edit pictures with incredible precision, restore old scans, and even tag faces or locations. These programs aren't required to organize your photos, but they can be a lot of fun to explore once you're comfortable.

If you prefer something simpler, you can stick with the built-in tools on your computer and still create an organized, beautiful library of memories. Many people find that having a large screen makes the entire experience more satisfying. Seeing your pictures full-size on a monitor can bring out details you'd never notice on a phone.

For those who don't use a computer every day, it's worth taking a little time to get comfortable with how files and folders work. Once you understand how to drag and drop files, rename folders, and use the mouse or trackpad, you'll find that organizing pictures becomes almost second nature.

Some people also enjoy combining the strengths of both tablets and computers. You might use your tablet for viewing, sharing, and light editing while relying on your computer for storage and backups. This combination lets you enjoy your photos wherever you are while keeping everything safe at home.

Using a tablet or computer gives you more control over your photos and helps you make sense of your collection. Instead of feeling at the mercy of whatever your phone decides to show you, you can create your own system, tailored to how you like to see and share your memories.

Connecting your devices together

Once you've grown more comfortable with your individual devices—your phone, camera, tablet, and computer—the next natural step is learning how to make them work together. This is where organizing your photos becomes much more seamless. Connecting your devices allows you to move pictures between them, back them up, and even view the same photo on multiple screens without having to hunt it down each time.

It helps to think of your devices as parts of the same team. Each one has its strengths. Your smartphone is your quick and convenient camera that's always in your pocket. Your digital camera gives you higher-quality pictures when you want them. Your tablet makes it easy to browse and share, and your computer gives you a home base where everything is stored and organized. Bringing them all into the same system means your memories are always at your fingertips, no matter which device you pick up.

The simplest connection between devices is a physical one. Plugging a cable from one to another can often do the job. If you want to transfer pictures from your phone to your computer, for example, you can use the charging cable that came with your phone. On an iPhone, plug the Lightning cable into your phone and the USB end into your computer. On an Android, the same idea applies, though the connector shape might be different. Your computer will usually recognize your phone and display it as a drive or folder where you can drag pictures over.

Your digital camera connects in a similar way, either directly via its USB cable or by removing the memory card and inserting it into your computer's card reader. This direct method is reliable and doesn't require any internet connection. If you prefer something familiar and hands-on, it's a good place to start.

For those who want to skip the cables, many modern devices also talk to each other wirelessly. This is where Wi-Fi and Bluetooth come in. Smartphones, tablets, and computers all have built-in wireless capabilities, and even some cameras now include them. With a home Wi-Fi network, you can log each of your devices onto the same network and allow them to communicate.

One common wireless method is using cloud services. If you turn on iCloud on your iPhone, tablet, and computer, all of your photos are stored in your iCloud account and automatically updated across every device logged into the same account. Similarly, Google Photos works with Android devices, tablets, and computers by logging in with the same Google account. This means you can take a photo on your phone, open your tablet a minute later, and see that photo already there.

For Windows computers, Microsoft offers OneDrive, which can also be installed on phones and tablets. Many people use Dropbox for the same reason—it works on nearly any device and keeps files synced. Choosing one cloud service and sticking with it makes the process much easier. Once set up, it's almost invisible. You don't have to think about transferring pictures because the devices keep themselves up to date.

There are also apps specifically made for transferring pictures between devices. Many camera manufacturers, like Canon, Nikon, and Sony, offer free apps that let you connect your camera directly to your phone or tablet via Wi-Fi or Bluetooth. These apps usually guide you through the connection process and let you transfer pictures on the spot. This is handy when you want to post a photo from your camera on social media without waiting until you're back at your computer.

Some people like to use external drives to move pictures between devices. A small USB flash drive or an external hard drive can hold thousands of photos and plug into any computer. If you have a newer tablet or phone with a USB port, there are also special flash drives that work with both computers and mobile devices. This gives you a portable way to carry your collection from one device to another.

It's also worth mentioning how these connections help keep your collection safe. When your photos exist in more than one place—your phone, your tablet, your computer, and the cloud—you reduce the risk of losing them if something happens to one device. This redundancy is one of the biggest benefits of connecting your devices.

Another advantage of linking your devices is that you can enjoy your photos in more ways. Many smart TVs now let you connect your phone, tablet, or computer and display your pictures on a big screen. This can be wonderful for family gatherings or simply for enjoying a slideshow of a recent trip from the comfort of your living room.

Tips on charging, cords, and Wi-Fi

Keeping your devices charged and connected is what makes everything you've learned so far actually work in day-to-day life. Whether you're snapping pictures with your phone, transferring them to your computer, or backing them up to the cloud, none of it happens if your battery is dead, the cords are in the wrong place, or the Wi-Fi isn't cooperating. These little details are easy to overlook, but getting comfortable with them removes a lot of unnecessary frustration.

Let's start with charging, because low batteries tend to appear at the least convenient moment—right when you're about to take a photo you don't want to miss. Every digital device you own runs on electricity stored in its battery, and most of these batteries are rechargeable. That means you don't have to replace them regularly; you just need to plug in the device and give it time to fill back up.

Phones, tablets, and many cameras come with their own charging cable when you first buy them. Each has its own connector shape, and it helps to keep them straight. For iPhones and iPads, the connector is called a Lightning cable. Newer iPhones and iPads are beginning to switch to USB-C, which is a small oval-shaped plug that's also found on many Android devices and laptops. Most Android phones and tablets use USB-C as well, though a few older ones still use the slightly larger Micro-USB.

Labeling your cords is one of the best habits you can develop. A small piece of masking tape on each plug, marked with the name of the device it belongs to, saves a lot of guessing later. You can even buy little colored tags or ties made for this purpose. Keeping cords organized in a drawer or a box, rather than scattered around the house, helps make sure you can always find what you need when it's time to charge.

Another good practice is to check the charging port of your device every now and then. Pocket lint, dust, or dirt can collect there over time and interfere with charging. A soft, dry toothbrush or a can of compressed air can gently clean it out if you notice the cable doesn't seem to fit properly or charging takes longer than usual.

It's also worth noting that you don't need to let your battery completely run down before recharging. In fact, modern rechargeable batteries tend to last longer if you keep them between about 20% and 80% most of the time. Plug in your device when it gets low, and don't stress about "over-charging"—your phone or tablet will stop charging itself once it's full.

Cameras often have removable batteries that need to be charged outside the camera in a little dock that comes with it. Keeping a second battery on hand is a good idea if you use your camera often. That way you can always have one charging while you're using the other.

Cords are not just for charging. Many of the cables that come with your devices are also used for transferring pictures to your computer or connecting to other devices. This is where knowing which cord belongs to which device really pays off. USB cables are the most common type, and many work interchangeably if they have the same ends, but it's always best to use the one that came with your device or one designed for it.

If you want to keep your cords from getting tangled or damaged, you can buy inexpensive cord wraps or use twist ties. Avoid bending them sharply or pulling them out by the cord instead of the plug. Treating them gently extends their life and saves you money.

Moving on to Wi-Fi—this is the invisible thread that links your devices together and gives them access to the internet. Without it, cloud backups won't happen, photos won't sync automatically, and sharing pictures by email or social media can become much harder.

Wi-Fi is just a wireless network your devices can join. If you already have it set up at home, all you need to do is connect each device to it once, and it will remember for next time. On your phone or tablet, go to Settings, find Wi-Fi, and choose your home network from the list. You'll have to enter the password, which is often printed on a sticker on your router or written down somewhere nearby. Once it's entered, your device will stay connected as long as it's in range.

On a computer, the process is much the same. In the corner of your screen, there's usually a little icon that looks like radio waves or a small fan shape. Click on it, select your network, and type in the password. If you have trouble connecting, restarting your router or calling your internet service provider can usually solve the problem.

One of the most common mistakes people make with Wi-Fi is trying to transfer or back up large batches of photos when the signal is weak. If your router is in another room or your signal is low, things may feel slow or fail altogether. Moving closer to the router or investing in a range extender can make a big difference.

You don't have to leave Wi-Fi on all the time if you're not using it, but it doesn't hurt to keep it connected whenever you're home. That way your devices can keep backing up your pictures and syncing across accounts without you having to think about it.

Public Wi-Fi at coffee shops, airports, and hotels can also work in a pinch, but keep in mind that these networks aren't as secure. It's fine to check your pictures or share a few, but it's better to save sensitive work like backing up your whole library for your home network.

3

GATHERING YOUR PHOTOS IN ONE PLACE

One of the most common frustrations people feel when trying to organize their digital photos is the sense of constantly finding more of them scattered everywhere—on old phones, memory cards in drawers, a cloud account they forgot they set up years ago. Starting to organize before you know what you're working with often leads to duplicated effort, missed memories, and a feeling of being stuck. Gathering everything first brings clarity. It turns what feels messy and endless into something you can actually see and work with, step by step.

Think of this stage as clearing the table before you start sorting a puzzle. Without all the pieces in front of you, you can't see the full picture. That's exactly what collecting your photos first does—it helps you understand the scope of your collection and sets you up to make thoughtful decisions later.

Digital photos are easy to accumulate without noticing. A single event, like a family vacation, might leave copies of the same pictures on your camera, your phone, your spouse's phone, and maybe even on a tablet or a social media account. Over the years, this multiplies into thousands of files, and it's easy to lose track of what's where. Gathering everything into one place before you start organizing prevents you from wasting time sorting the same batch twice or accidentally deleting something you wanted to keep.

One of the first benefits you'll notice once you've collected everything is how much easier it becomes to spot duplicates. Seeing two, three, or even five versions of the same photo in different folders or on different devices is normal. But if you're only looking at one device at a time, you might not realize duplicates exist. Bringing everything into one central place helps you recognize what's truly unique and what can be deleted or merged.

Collecting first also protects your memories. While it's tempting to dive into deleting and renaming right away, moving photos into a single folder or drive before making changes means you have a safety net. It's much easier to back up your entire collection at this stage, knowing you have one master set of files, before you begin to make decisions about what stays and what goes.

There's another, less obvious benefit to collecting everything up front: it helps you see patterns. Looking through pictures from different years and devices side by side can reveal themes in your life you hadn't noticed. You might rediscover moments you'd forgotten or spot gaps you'd like to fill by scanning printed photos or asking family members for their copies. The simple act of seeing your memories gathered in one place is often rewarding all by itself.

The process of collecting also gives you a chance to revisit old devices and accounts you might otherwise forget. Many people still have old smartphones tucked away in a drawer, cameras with full memory cards, or even an email inbox filled with photos they've sent to themselves over the years. Making a list of every place your photos might live—and checking each one—can feel satisfying. It's like recovering pieces of your story you didn't realize were missing.

It's worth taking your time during this stage. Rushing through and skipping devices or accounts only leaves you with more work later. Set a goal of checking one or two sources a day if that feels more manageable. Over a week or two, you'll likely gather the bulk of your photos without feeling overwhelmed.

While you're collecting, it's a good idea to create a single folder on your computer or external drive labeled something simple, like "All Photos To Sort." Everything you find—whether from your phone, tablet, camera, or cloud account

—can go into this folder. Even if the files have messy names or strange folders at this point, that's fine. The goal here is to gather, not organize.

This step is also when you might discover photos that belong to others in your family. It's common to find pictures from weddings, holidays, or vacations stored on someone else's phone or account. Reaching out to family members and letting them know you're collecting and organizing can be a nice way to involve them. They might send you photos you didn't even know existed.

Another thing to keep in mind while collecting is how you're naming and tracking your sources. It's helpful to jot down which devices and accounts you've already checked and which still need attention. That way you don't miss anything, and you also won't waste time checking the same place twice.

Collecting everything first also reduces the stress of decision-making. Many people feel paralyzed by the thought of deciding what to keep or delete when they're only halfway through finding all their pictures. When you know you have everything in one place, you can move on to organizing with confidence.

How to find photos on your phone

Phones have become the most common way to take pictures, yet they're also where many people lose track of what they've taken. It's not unusual to feel like your photos have slipped into some invisible corner of your device, leaving you scrolling endlessly or giving up before you find what you're looking for. Learning how to quickly find photos on your phone can make all the difference in enjoying your memories instead of feeling frustrated by them.

Both iPhones and Android phones are designed to make photos easy to access, but the way they do it can feel confusing if you're not familiar with their systems. Once you know where to look and which options to use, however, you'll find that locating even an older photo becomes surprisingly simple.

Start by looking for the Photos app. Every phone has one, and it's usually right on the home screen when you unlock your phone. On iPhones, the app is simply called *Photos*, with an icon that looks like a colorful flower. On Android phones, it might also be called *Photos* if you're using Google Photos, or it may be labeled *Gallery*. Both apps do the same thing: they collect all your pictures in one place.

When you open the app, you're taken straight into your photo library. By default, it shows your pictures in chronological order, with the newest ones at the bottom. You can scroll up to go back in time and down to return to your latest shots. Many people overlook this simple timeline and instead scroll quickly, which can make you miss what you're looking for. Try scrolling more slowly, paying attention to the dates that sometimes appear as you move through the gallery.

On an iPhone, you can also tap the *Albums* button at the bottom of the screen. This takes you to a list of organized folders the phone creates for you. There's usually an album called *Recents*, which contains everything you've taken or saved. You may also see other albums labeled *Favorites*, *Videos*, *Screenshots*, or even ones created automatically for people, places, or pets. These can be very helpful if you're trying to find a specific type of photo.

On an Android, the *Albums* tab works similarly. It often lists folders by where the picture came from—your camera, downloads, messaging apps, or even screenshots. If you received a picture in a text or saved one from email, it usually ends up in one of these specific folders. Checking these can save you from thinking a photo has disappeared when it's just been placed in a different album.

Another feature worth getting to know is the search function. On both iPhones and Android phones, the Photos app includes a magnifying glass icon or a *Search* bar at the top. This lets you type in keywords like "beach," "birthday," or even a person's name if you've tagged them before. The phone uses image recognition to pull up pictures it thinks match your word. This is especially handy if you can't remember when the photo was taken but you know what was in it.

If you've backed your photos up to the cloud—using

iCloud on iPhone or Google Photos on Android—the search function becomes even more powerful because it can look through your entire cloud library, not just what's stored on the phone itself. This also means you may see photos from older devices as long as they've been uploaded to your account.

Another helpful tip is to use the *Favorites* feature while you're browsing. If you find a picture you know you'll want to return to often, tap the heart icon on iPhone or the star icon on Android. This adds it to your Favorites album, which you can access anytime without scrolling through your entire library.

If you're trying to find photos someone else sent you, it's worth checking the messaging app you use. On iPhone, open the *Messages* app, tap the conversation with that person, and then tap their name at the top of the screen. You'll see an option labeled *Photos*, which displays every picture shared in that conversation. On Android, the process is similar—open your messaging app, tap on the conversation, and look for the media gallery that collects shared images.

One common issue people run into is that photos they thought they took are no longer on their phone. This often happens when the phone runs out of storage and moves older photos to the cloud to save space. If you see a picture in your library but it takes a moment to load when you tap on it, that's a sign it's stored in the cloud. As long as you're connected to Wi-Fi or mobile data, it should still load, though it might take a little longer.

If you're not finding what you're looking for, it's also a good idea to check apps other than the default Photos or Gallery. Apps like WhatsApp, Facebook, and Instagram often save copies of photos you've shared or downloaded within their own folders. You can usually find these by opening the app and looking at your own profile or by checking the Albums tab in your main photo app for folders named after those services.

Downloading from email or text messages

As more and more of our photos arrive digitally—rather than in an envelope or album from the corner store—being able to download them properly from email and text messages has become an essential skill. Family and friends often send pictures this way, whether it's a snapshot of last weekend's barbecue, a photo of a new baby, or a scanned copy of an old wedding portrait. You might glance at these pictures when they come in and feel happy to see them, but unless you download them, they can easily slip away, buried under newer messages. Learning how to save photos from email and text messages gives you control over those memories, letting you keep them where you'll actually find and enjoy them later.

On your phone, photos sent by text message are handled

slightly differently from those sent by email, but they have something in common: neither saves the picture into your photo library automatically. This is a detail many people don't realize at first. Just seeing the photo doesn't mean it's stored on your device yet. Until you actively save it, it remains part of the message conversation or email thread and won't show up in your Albums or cloud backup.

Let's start with text messages. On an iPhone, if you open your *Messages* app and tap on a conversation, you can scroll back to any picture that's been sent to you. When you see the photo you want to save, press your finger lightly on it and hold. A menu will appear with several options, including *Save Image*. Tap *Save Image*, and the photo is instantly copied into your Photos app. You can double-check by leaving Messages, opening Photos, and looking in your *Recents* album. That picture should now appear there.

On Android phones, the process is similar but sometimes the wording is a little different. Open the messaging app and find the conversation that contains the photo you'd like to keep. Tap on the photo, and you may see an icon in the corner like three dots or a downward arrow. Tap that icon, and choose *Save* or *Download*. Again, the photo is then stored in your Gallery or Photos app.

One helpful tip is to review entire conversations every now and then to make sure you haven't missed any photos. Sometimes people send multiple pictures over time, and it's easy to forget you've only saved a few. Both iPhone and

Android let you view all the photos in a single conversation at once. On an iPhone, open the conversation, tap the name of the person at the top of the screen, then scroll down to see *Photos*. On Android, in most messaging apps, there's a similar section, often called *Media* or *View all.*

Now let's talk about email. Saving photos from email works a little differently, but it's just as straightforward once you know where to tap. On an iPhone, open the *Mail* app and find the message that contains the photo. You'll usually see the photo embedded in the body of the email or as an attachment at the bottom. If it's embedded, press and hold your finger on the photo, then tap *Save Image*. If it's listed as an attachment, tap to open it first, then use the same press-and-hold gesture to save it. The photo will go into your Photos app just like one saved from a text message.

On Android phones, open your email app—usually Gmail or another mail client—and find the email. If the picture is embedded, press and hold, then choose *Download* or *Save to Gallery*. If the photo is an attachment, there's often a little download icon next to it you can tap. Again, this saves it to your phone's main photo gallery.

Sometimes people send more than one photo in an email. If you're on a computer, this is even easier to handle. Open the email, and you'll usually see each photo listed or displayed. Many email programs will offer a single *Download All* option that saves everything at once into a folder on your computer. You can then move these photos into your main photo storage, external drive, or cloud service when you're ready.

There's one small detail to watch for when downloading from email: sometimes emails include low-quality previews of the pictures to make the message load faster. Always tap or click on the photo to open it fully before you save it, to ensure you're downloading the full-resolution version rather than a blurry thumbnail.

Another habit that helps is renaming your photos after you download them. This isn't something you have to do right away, but if you save a picture from an email and it's just named something like "IMG_4567," it can be hard to know what it is later. Adding even a simple name like "Emma's Birthday 2023" makes it easier to find later.

If you regularly receive photos from the same person, consider creating a folder or album for them as you download. This helps you keep related photos together instead of scattering them throughout your main library. On both iPhone and Android, you can create albums directly in the Photos app and add pictures as you save them.

Some email services also include automatic saving features. For example, if someone emails you a photo and you use Gmail with Google Photos, the attachment may already appear in Google Photos without you doing anything extra—provided you've enabled the setting that links your Google account with Google Photos. This is worth checking if you use Gmail.

The key idea to remember when working with photos sent to you is that nothing happens automatically unless you set it up that way. If you want the photo to be part of your permanent library and included in your backups, you need to take a moment to download or save it. That single step is what makes the difference between a memory you can easily find later and one that's buried in an old email or text thread you might never think to check again.

Transferring from your camera or memory card

Many people still prefer the feel of a real camera in their hands. Even with the popularity of smartphones, cameras remain a favorite tool for special occasions and trips, thanks to their higher-quality lenses and better control over settings. If you've used a digital camera to capture moments that matter to you, knowing how to transfer those pictures onto your computer or main storage is an important step. Pictures left sitting on a memory card can be forgotten, and worse, they risk being lost if the card fails. Fortunately, transferring from a camera or memory card is simple once you understand the process.

Your camera doesn't actually store pictures forever—it just holds them on a tiny memory card until you move them somewhere more permanent. These cards, called SD cards (or sometimes microSD if they're smaller), are removable and can be inserted into computers, card readers, or even some printers. Many cameras also include a cord you can use to connect the whole camera directly to your computer if you prefer not to handle the card itself.

Let's start with the memory card method, since it tends to be the most straightforward. First, turn off your camera and locate the compartment where the card lives. Usually it's behind a little door on the side or bottom of the camera. Press gently on the card and it should pop out slightly, allowing you to slide it free. If your card is very small and hard to grip, don't worry—there are inexpensive adapters that make handling microSD cards easier.

Next, check your computer to see if it has a card slot built in. Many laptops and desktop towers include a thin slot that's just the right size for a standard SD card. Slide the card into this slot with the label facing up (or whatever orientation your computer requires; it's often printed next to the slot). The computer will recognize the card as if it were an external drive, and a window usually appears on the screen showing the contents. If a window doesn't pop up automatically, you can open your file browser—called *File Explorer* on Windows or *Finder* on Mac—and look for a drive labeled something like "No Name," "Untitled," or the brand of your card.

Once you can see the files, it's just a matter of copying them to the place you want to store them. Many people find it helpful to create a folder on the computer first, labeled with the date or event. For example, "June 2025 – Grandkids Visit." Then you can select the photos from the memory card, drag them into your folder, and let the computer do the copying.

If your computer doesn't have a built-in card slot, don't worry. You can buy a small external card reader that plugs into a USB port. These are inexpensive, and they work the same way. You insert the card into the reader, plug the reader into your computer, and the files appear just as if you'd used a built-in slot.

The other option is connecting the camera itself with its included cable. Most cameras come with a USB cable that plugs into the camera at one end and your computer at the other. With this method, you don't need to remove the memory card at all. Once plugged in, the camera will often display a message asking if you want to connect to a computer. Choose yes, and again, your computer should recognize it as an external drive or camera. Then you can copy the files the same way as with the memory card.

One small note: if you use the cable method, make sure your camera has enough battery power to stay on during the transfer. Some cameras won't work properly if the battery is low. If you find the camera shuts off halfway through, try charging it first or switching to the card method.

When transferring your photos, it's a good idea to copy them rather than move them. Copying leaves the original files on the memory card as a backup until you're sure everything transferred correctly. Once you've confirmed that the pictures are safely on your computer and backed up to your main storage, you can delete them from the card to free up space.

Sometimes cameras create folders with unfamiliar names like "DCIM" or "100CANON." Don't be confused by this—it's just how cameras organize files internally. Your pictures will still be inside those folders, and you can move them out and rename them as you wish on your computer.

If you like to keep things tidy, you might also want to rename the files themselves. Camera file names are usually something like "IMG_2345," which isn't very helpful when you're trying to find pictures later. Renaming them to include a date or subject—such as "2025-06-Grandkids-Visit-1"—can make a big difference down the road.

If your camera shoots in a format other than JPG, you might notice some files don't open right away on your computer. This is because some cameras offer "RAW" files, which are larger and meant for professional editing. If you don't plan to do heavy editing, it's fine to stick with the JPG files, which are universally readable.

Finding pictures already on your computer

Many people feel surprised by just how many photos they already have sitting quietly on their computer. Years of downloading email attachments, plugging in memory cards, saving texted images, and even transferring from old cameras can leave dozens of folders full of pictures hiding in plain sight. If you've ever thought, *I know that photo's here somewhere... but where?*, you're not alone. Taking the time to locate and gather what you already have on your computer is one of the smartest moves you can make before organizing. It gives you a clear starting point and prevents you from creating unnecessary duplicates later.

The first thing to understand is that computers don't usually scatter your photos randomly—though it can sometimes feel that way. Instead, they put them in default folders, often named things like *Pictures*, *Downloads*, or *Documents*. The challenge is that you might have saved a few to each over the years without realizing it.

Start by opening your file manager. On a Windows computer, this is called *File Explorer*. You can usually find its yellow folder icon at the bottom of your screen or by clicking the Start button and typing "File Explorer" in the search box. On a Mac, your file manager is called *Finder*, and its smiling blue face icon is always sitting on the bottom left of your screen.

Once your file manager is open, the simplest place to begin is your *Pictures* folder. On Windows, you'll see it listed on the left-hand panel under "This PC" or "Quick Access." On a Mac, it's under your home folder. Open it up, and you may find a treasure trove of pictures you didn't even know you still had. Some may be organized into folders named after events or years if you—or your camera—set them up that way. Others might all sit in one big list. Either way, take note of what's there.

Next, check your *Downloads* folder. This is where your computer saves files when you download them from email, social media, or the web. You'll often find individual pictures here, sometimes with generic names like "image001.jpg" or "photo.jpg." It's easy to forget about these because the folder can fill up quickly and push older files out of sight. Scroll through carefully—you may be surprised by what you find.

On Windows computers, there's another helpful tool called the search bar. It sits at the top-right corner of File Explorer. Type in common photo file extensions like .jpg, .png, or .heic (the kind of files your phone and camera create). Press Enter, and your computer will scan the folder you're looking at—or even the whole hard drive if you prefer—and display every file with that extension. This is one of the fastest ways to uncover pictures tucked away in unexpected places.

Mac users can do the same thing with Spotlight search. Press the Command key and the space bar at the same time, and a search box will appear. Type in .jpg or .png and see what comes up. You can also open Finder and use the search box in the top-right corner to look for all image files at once.

If you've ever used photo management software, like Apple Photos, Google Backup and Sync, or Windows Photo Gallery, you may already have a library that's been gathering your pictures in the background. On a Mac, open the *Photos* app (you'll find it in your Applications folder or dock) and let it load. It may already show you years' worth of pictures organized by date or album. On a Windows computer, search for the *Photos* app in the Start menu—it works much the same way, though the layout is slightly different.

Sometimes, you may find pictures saved in places you wouldn't think to look—like your *Documents* folder or even your Desktop. People often save or drag photos there temporarily and forget to move them later. It can help to check these spots while you're gathering everything together.

If you've used external drives or USB sticks in the past, now is also a good time to plug them in and see what's there. Many people use these to offload photos when their computer's storage fills up, and then forget they even have them. Once plugged in, they'll appear as an extra drive in File Explorer or Finder, and you can browse them the same way.

For those who have used cloud services—like Google Drive, Dropbox, or OneDrive—you can also log into those accounts on your web browser and check whether you've saved any pictures there. Many people don't realize that apps and services sometimes back up photos automatically if you agreed to it when setting them up. Download any pictures you want to keep onto your computer so they're part of your main library.

As you go through this process, it's helpful to set up a single folder on your desktop or external drive called something like *Photos To Organize*. Any pictures you find, no matter where they're hiding, can be copied into this folder. Don't worry yet about sorting them into albums or renaming them—just get them all into one place so you can see what you're working with.

You might find multiple copies of the same picture, which is perfectly normal. Don't delete anything yet; that's a later step. For now, focus on gathering. Even if two copies have slightly different names or sizes, you'll want to compare them side by side later to decide which to keep.

What to do with printed photos

Printed photographs hold a kind of magic. There's something about holding a picture in your hands, seeing the colors and the paper's texture, that brings a memory to life in a way a screen never quite matches. Many people have boxes, albums, or even entire drawers filled with prints from decades past—school portraits, vacation snapshots, baby pictures, holiday gatherings. While these prints are precious, they can also be vulnerable to fading, tearing, or simply getting lost.

One of the biggest challenges is figuring out what role those prints play alongside your growing digital collection. There's no single right answer, but a few thoughtful choices can help you protect those memories and bring them into your more modern organization system, if you'd like.

Start by taking a good look at what you already have.

Many printed photo collections have been sitting untouched for years. Pull them out of closets, drawers, or boxes and lay them out on a table where you can really see them. Don't worry about sorting yet; the first step is simply to become familiar with what you're working with.

You may notice right away that some pictures have held up better than others. Older prints, especially those made before the 1990s, tend to fade or yellow over time. Others may have curled edges or even stuck to the pages of those old sticky-backed albums. The goal at this stage isn't to restore or repair anything, but it is worth identifying any prints that feel especially fragile so you can handle them with care.

As you review your printed collection, think about which pictures mean the most to you. Many of us keep every single print we've ever received, but not every picture tells a story worth preserving. You might find three or four nearly identical shots of the same birthday party or a stack of blurry vacation landscapes. Just like with digital photos, it's perfectly fine to set aside duplicates or unimportant shots. You don't have to throw them away if you're not ready, but separating them can make the rest of your collection feel more manageable.

Once you have a sense of which prints matter most, you can decide how to store and display them. For those you'd like to keep in their physical form, archival-quality photo boxes and acid-free albums are the best way to protect them from further damage. Regular cardboard and paper can actually contribute to fading and deterioration over time, but archival supplies are designed to keep photos safe for years. Labeling the backs of prints or the dividers in your boxes with names and dates also helps preserve the context for future generations.

If you'd rather not have stacks of prints taking up space—or if you want to share them more easily—you can also choose to digitize them. This means creating digital copies of your printed photos by scanning them. Scanning can feel intimidating if you've never done it before, but it's more straightforward than you might think.

There are several ways to scan printed photos. If you already have a printer with a flatbed scanner at home, that's a perfectly good place to start. Place one or two prints face-down on the glass, close the lid, and press the scan button. Most scanners give you the choice of saving the image to your computer, where you can then move it into your photo library alongside your other digital pictures.

If you don't own a scanner—or if you have a large number of prints to work through—there are other options. Many office supply stores and copy centers offer scanning services. You can bring in a stack of photos, and they'll scan them for you, sometimes even saving them to a flash drive or uploading them to a cloud account. There are also specialty services that will handle large or delicate collections, even restoring faded colors or fixing minor damage digitally.

For a faster, more casual approach, you can even use your

smartphone to create digital copies of prints. Apps like Google PhotoScan or even your phone's built-in camera can capture surprisingly good images when used carefully. Lay the print on a flat, well-lit surface, avoid casting shadows, and take your time to line up the edges. While this method may not produce professional-level results, it's an excellent way to quickly digitize family memories for sharing online or backing up.

If you choose to scan your prints, it's worth thinking about how you'll organize the digital versions as you go. Scanning can quickly create dozens—or even hundreds—of files, which can feel overwhelming if you don't have a plan. Naming each file with a clear description and date (if you know it) can save you hours of frustration later. You might use a structure like "1965-Christmas-Dinner-01.jpg" to keep things consistent.

You may also want to keep a record of where the original print is stored, just in case you ever need to reference it again. Some people like to create a little inventory document that lists what's been scanned and where the physical copy is located.

One of the biggest benefits of scanning printed photos is the peace of mind it brings. Once you have a digital copy, you can include it in your regular backups, ensuring that even if the original print is damaged or lost, the memory itself isn't gone. You can also share digital versions more easily with family and friends, many of whom may never have seen these older pictures before.

For those who feel unsure about parting with the physical prints after scanning, remember that you don't have to. Many people choose to keep their most meaningful prints in albums or frames, while storing less important ones in labeled boxes just in case. The point isn't to get rid of the past —it's to make sure you can enjoy and protect it.

4

CHOOSING WHERE TO STORE YOUR PHOTOS

The term "cloud" can sound vague, mysterious, or even intimidating when you first hear it. For many people, the word conjures up the image of something floating far away and out of reach. Yet in reality, the cloud is simply another place to store your digital photos, and it can actually make your life much easier. Understanding what the cloud really is—and how it works—can help you feel more comfortable using it to protect and access your pictures.

At its simplest, the cloud refers to computer servers connected to the internet. These servers belong to companies like Apple, Google, Microsoft, or Amazon, and they are designed to store and protect your digital files. Instead of keeping everything only on your own phone, tablet, or computer, you can upload copies of your photos to these servers through an internet connection. Once your photos are there, you can access them from almost anywhere, on nearly any device, simply by logging into your account.

Think of the cloud as a kind of virtual storage room that you rent from a company. You don't have to build or maintain the room yourself, and you can visit it anytime. Even if your own computer breaks or your phone is lost, the files you've placed in the cloud are still safe and waiting for you. This is one of the main reasons why the cloud has become such a popular way to store and back up photos.

Many people's first question is: where, physically, are my pictures when they're "in the cloud"? They are actually stored on hard drives inside enormous, highly secure buildings called data centers. These centers are located all over the world, but you don't need to know their exact addresses. The cloud service you choose takes care of that, managing the servers and making sure your photos stay available to you whenever you want them. It's like mailing your photographs to a trusted, professional archivist who keeps them organized and ready whenever you ask.

One of the greatest advantages of using the cloud is that it connects seamlessly with your other devices. If you take a picture on your phone, it can automatically upload to the cloud without you having to do anything. Later, you can log into your tablet, computer, or even someone else's device, and see that same picture there too. This makes it easy to share photos, show them to family during a visit, or even print them out somewhere else.

Many people also worry about whether the cloud is safe. The short answer is yes—as safe as modern technology allows. Companies that run cloud services use advanced security systems to keep your photos private and protected from hackers or accidental loss. Of course, nothing in life is 100 percent guaranteed, but in most cases, your photos are much safer in the cloud than if they only live on your phone, which could be dropped, stolen, or damaged.

You might already be using the cloud without realizing it. If you use an iPhone or iPad, Apple automatically offers a service called iCloud. If you use an Android phone, Google Photos is usually included. Both of these are cloud services. If you log into your Apple or Google account and see your pictures waiting for you there, you're already using the cloud.

People often wonder whether the cloud is free. Many companies offer a small amount of free storage—enough to hold thousands of pictures for many people. However, if you take lots of photos or also want to store videos, you might eventually fill up that free space. At that point, the company will offer to sell you more space, usually for a modest monthly fee. Think of it as paying for an extra shelf in that virtual storage room. The good news is that you don't have to decide right away. You can start with the free space, see how it works, and then choose to upgrade only if you really need it.

Another question people ask is: do I still "own" my pictures if they're in the cloud? The answer is absolutely yes. The cloud is just a service to store and deliver your files. You still have full ownership of your photos, and you can download them back to your computer or phone anytime you like. Think of the cloud as an extra copy, not a replacement. It's a backup—a way to make sure your memories survive even if something happens to your local devices.

Using the cloud also helps you stay organized. Many cloud services automatically sort your photos by date, location, or even the people in them. You can search for a photo just by typing something like "beach" or "Christmas," and it will show you the matching pictures almost instantly. This can save you hours of scrolling through folders on your computer.

Pros and cons of cloud storage

One of the biggest benefits of cloud storage is its ability to keep your photos safe from the most common mishaps. Computers can crash, hard drives can fail, and phones can be dropped or lost. When your pictures are backed up in the cloud, you don't have to worry as much about losing everything if your device stops working. That peace of mind is hard to overstate. Even in the worst-case scenario, your pictures are still waiting for you online, ready to be downloaded to a new device when you're ready.

Another strength of the cloud is how accessible it makes your photos. Once your pictures are stored there, you can view them from almost anywhere. Sitting on your sofa with a tablet, visiting family and using their computer, or even just scrolling on your phone while waiting at the doctor's office—you can log in to your account and bring up your whole library. That flexibility is especially helpful when you want to share pictures with friends and relatives. You don't need to carry a stack of prints or hunt through folders. Instead, a few taps or clicks and your memories appear.

The cloud also has a way of keeping things organized. Many services automatically sort your pictures by date, location, or even who's in them. You can search for specific moments without having to scroll endlessly. For example, typing in "beach" might bring up all the beach vacations you've taken over the years. This kind of built-in organization can save time and make your collection feel more manageable.

Space is another factor to consider. Phones and computers have limited storage, and digital photos—especially if you have many—can quickly fill up that space. The cloud gives you extra room to keep more pictures without having to worry about deleting older ones to make space for new ones. Even the free plans from most services can hold thousands of pictures. If your collection is larger, you can usually buy more storage for a modest monthly fee.

On the flip side, there are a few drawbacks you should

weigh. The most obvious is that the cloud requires an internet connection. If your connection is slow or unreliable, uploading and accessing your pictures might feel frustrating at times. Even though you can view pictures already downloaded to your phone or computer, accessing your entire cloud library depends on being online.

Cost is another factor. While the basic free plans can be plenty for some, others find they need more storage than the free tier allows. Paying a monthly or annual fee isn't always a burden, but it is one more bill to keep in mind. Some people also feel uneasy about being "locked in" to one company's ecosystem—if you switch services later, transferring everything can take time and effort.

Privacy is a concern for some, too. While reputable cloud companies use strong security to keep your photos safe, you're still trusting them with your memories. Most services do not look through or use your pictures for any purpose beyond storage, but it's natural to feel a little hesitant about uploading personal family photos to someone else's servers. Reading the privacy policy of whichever service you choose can help you feel more confident.

Speed can also be a consideration. Uploading a large collection of photos for the first time might take several hours—or even days—depending on the size of your library and the speed of your internet. Once they're up there, though, accessing them tends to be much faster.

For people who like to have a sense of control, the cloud

can sometimes feel a little too "invisible." With an external hard drive, you can hold it in your hand and know exactly where your photos live. With the cloud, everything is digital, and that lack of a physical object can make some people feel uneasy. It can help to think of the cloud as one more layer of backup, rather than the only place your photos live.

Another potential issue is that no technology is perfect. While rare, there have been occasional service outages when a company's servers go down for a short time. Usually, everything is restored quickly and no data is lost, but it's worth knowing that temporary disruptions can happen.

For many people, the best approach is to use the cloud alongside another form of storage. That way, you get the convenience and safety of cloud access while still keeping a backup on an external drive or even on your computer. Having your pictures in more than one place is a smart way to protect them against all kinds of problems—whether it's a broken phone, a technical glitch, or an accidental deletion.

Another advantage worth mentioning is how easy the cloud makes it to share memories with others. If you'd like to show your grandchildren what their parents looked like as kids, or send your friend a copy of that great photo from a reunion, it's as simple as sending them a link. You can even set up shared albums where everyone adds their pictures from the same event, creating a complete collection everyone can enjoy.

As you think about whether the cloud is right for you, it

helps to consider what matters most in your situation. If having access to your pictures from anywhere is important, or if you feel nervous about losing your phone or computer, the cloud is a strong option. If you prefer knowing exactly where your files are stored, or if you're on a very slow or limited internet connection, you might lean more heavily on physical storage instead.

You don't have to choose one or the other exclusively. Many people start with a free cloud account to test it out and then expand or adjust as their needs grow. You can also experiment with a few different services before settling on the one you like best. Since all the major services work on both computers and phones, you can pick the one that feels easiest to use and offers the features you care about most.

Storing on your computer or external drive

Many people feel more comfortable keeping their digital photos somewhere they can see and control directly. For those who prefer a hands-on approach to managing their memories, storing photos on your own computer or an external hard drive can feel reassuring. Knowing your pictures are right there, saved in a place you can touch and open yourself, gives a certain peace of mind that digital clouds don't always provide.

One of the biggest advantages of keeping photos on your computer is convenience. When they're saved locally, you don't need an internet connection to view them, organize them, or share them. As soon as you turn on your machine, everything is at your fingertips. For those who don't always have reliable internet—or who prefer not to depend on it—this can be a major benefit.

If your computer has enough storage space, you can keep your entire library right on the hard drive. Most modern computers come with hundreds of gigabytes of space, which can hold tens of thousands of photos. The key to making this work well is keeping your files organized. Create a dedicated folder just for your pictures, and use clearly named subfolders for years, events, or people. This not only helps you find what you're looking for but also makes it easier to back up your photos when the time comes.

One downside of storing everything on your computer is that hard drives can and do fail. Even new computers can experience problems, and older ones are more likely to develop issues over time. That's why it's a good idea not to rely on your computer alone. You can complement it by saving copies of your pictures to an external hard drive.

An external drive is simply a separate storage device that plugs into your computer. They come in many shapes and sizes, but all serve the same purpose: giving you extra space and a secure backup. Some are small enough to fit in your pocket, while others are about the size of a book. They usually connect to your computer with a USB cable, and once plugged in, they show up as another drive in your file manager.

Copying photos to an external drive is as easy as dragging and dropping them into folders, just like you do on your computer. Many people use their external drive as a complete mirror of their photo library, keeping everything neatly backed up. Others use it to store older pictures they don't look at often but still want to keep safe.

One advantage of external drives is their portability. You can unplug one and take it with you or store it somewhere separate from your computer. That way, if anything happens to your computer—like a fire, theft, or accidental damage—your pictures are still safe elsewhere.

It's worth noting that not all external drives are the same. There are two main types: traditional hard drives (often called HDDs) and solid-state drives (SSDs). HDDs are usually less expensive and offer more storage for the money, but they have moving parts that can wear out over time. SSDs are faster and more durable because they don't have moving parts, though they tend to cost a little more per gigabyte. Either type will serve you well for photos, so the choice comes down to your budget and personal preference.

Some external drives even come with software that can automatically back up your computer on a schedule. This feature can save time and help make sure you never forget to update your backup. Once set up, you can simply plug in your drive every week or month and let the program do its work.

One thing to keep in mind is that external drives, like computers, are not immune to problems. They can also fail or be lost. For maximum safety, it's a good idea to keep more than one copy of your photos—on your computer, on an external drive, and optionally in the cloud as well. Having your memories in two or three places greatly reduces the chances of losing them forever.

For people who feel more comfortable with physical objects, external drives offer a satisfying sense of control. You can label them, keep them on a shelf or in a safe place, and always know where your pictures live. If you ever upgrade your computer or switch to a new one, it's easy to plug your external drive into the new machine and move your photos over without much fuss.

Another helpful habit is to keep your external drive organized just like your computer. Create folders with clear names, and try to keep the same structure on both. That way, you can always find what you're looking for, no matter which device you're using.

Some people also like to use more than one external drive, rotating between them. For example, you might back up your photos on one drive this month and on a second drive the next. Then you store one of them somewhere else, like a trusted family member's home or a safety deposit box.

This provides an extra layer of protection in case of accidents.

One additional benefit of using external drives is that they don't require ongoing payments. Unlike cloud services, where you may eventually have to pay for more space, you pay for an external drive once and use it as long as it lasts. Many drives work perfectly well for five years or more if handled carefully.

Popular cloud services

When you decide you're ready to try cloud storage, one of the first decisions you'll face is which service to use. It can feel like there are endless options, each with its own features, prices, and quirks. Choosing one doesn't have to be stressful, though. Four of the most widely used services—Google Photos, Apple iCloud, Amazon Photos, and Dropbox—are all solid choices, and each has strengths that may suit you better depending on your habits and the devices you already use.

Google Photos has become one of the most popular choices for storing pictures online, and it's easy to see why. If you already use an Android phone, chances are good that Google Photos is already on your device and quietly working in the background. One of its biggest advantages is how much it does automatically. When turned on, it backs up your photos in real time as you take them, without you having to think about it. You can then access your pictures from your phone, tablet, computer, or even someone else's device simply by logging into your Google account.

One standout feature of Google Photos is its powerful search. You can type in words like "dog," "sunset," or "wedding," and it will show you all your photos that match. It also organizes pictures by date and creates little "memories" collections that pop up and remind you of moments from years past. Google offers a generous amount of free storage, though as your collection grows you may need to purchase extra space. The paid plans are affordable, and you can expand gradually as needed. It works equally well on Windows and Mac computers, making it a good fit if you use a mix of devices.

Apple iCloud is another excellent choice, especially if you're already using an iPhone, iPad, or Mac. iCloud is deeply woven into Apple's ecosystem, and it feels very natural for anyone familiar with those devices. Once you turn on iCloud Photos, every photo you take with your iPhone or iPad is backed up automatically. You can view them on your other Apple devices instantly, and they're kept in perfect sync. Edit a picture on your iPad, and the change appears on your iPhone and Mac as well.

What makes iCloud particularly appealing is its seamless integration. You hardly have to think about it once it's set up. Your photo library looks the same no matter which Apple device you're using, which can feel reassuring and simple.

iCloud does charge for larger amounts of storage beyond the small free tier, but the pricing is clear and scales up depending on how much space you need. If you mainly use Apple products and value simplicity, iCloud often feels like the most natural choice.

Amazon Photos may not be as widely talked about as Google and Apple, but it has one big benefit if you're already an Amazon Prime member: unlimited photo storage. For people with a large collection, this can be a huge cost saver over time. Like the others, Amazon Photos offers automatic backups and organizes your pictures by date and album. Its app is available on all major platforms, including iPhone, Android, Windows, and Mac, making it a flexible choice.

One helpful feature Amazon offers is Family Vault, which lets you share your unlimited storage with up to five other people. This is particularly nice for families who want to pool their memories into one place without extra costs. Even if you're not a Prime member, Amazon Photos still offers paid plans at competitive rates, though the unlimited photo storage is exclusive to Prime subscribers. If you already use Amazon for shopping and streaming, it's worth checking if this benefit is included in your membership.

Dropbox, while slightly different from the others, is still a very good option for storing photos online. Originally designed as a general file storage service, Dropbox has evolved into a reliable way to keep pictures, documents, and other files safe and accessible. One of Dropbox's strengths is its simplicity—it works almost like a regular folder on your computer, and anything you put into it is synced to the cloud and to your other devices.

Dropbox doesn't have as many specialized photo features as Google or Apple, but it does allow you to organize pictures in your own way, and its sharing features are excellent. You can send friends and family direct links to albums or individual photos without them needing an account. It's also highly compatible with both Windows and Mac computers, as well as Android and iPhone. Dropbox does offer a free tier with limited space, but you may need to upgrade to a paid plan for larger libraries.

When deciding which service feels right for you, it can help to think about the devices you already use every day. If you're firmly in the Apple world, iCloud will likely feel the most natural. If you're an Android user or like Google's search and organization features, Google Photos might be more comfortable. If you already pay for Amazon Prime, taking advantage of unlimited photo storage with Amazon Photos could save you money. And if you prefer something simple and versatile for all kinds of files, Dropbox is a strong contender.

5

DELETING & DECLUTTERING

As you go through the process of organizing your digital photos, it can be tempting to keep everything. After all, storage feels endless, and deleting can feel final. But one of the most overlooked steps in creating a meaningful and manageable photo collection is letting go of the pictures that don't belong there. Deleting is not just about making space on a device. It's about clarity, focus, and making it easier for you to find and enjoy the moments that matter most.

When your photo library is full of duplicates, blurry shots, or forgettable images, finding the ones you actually care about becomes harder. Think about walking into a room packed to the ceiling with boxes. You know your favorite keepsakes are in there somewhere, but the sheer amount of clutter makes them almost impossible to find. Your photo library can feel the same way. Too much noise can drown out the music of your memories.

There's also a psychological benefit to curating your photos. Scrolling through a disorganized, overcrowded gallery can feel overwhelming and even stressful. It's not uncommon to open your phone or computer and think, "I'll never be able to sort through all this." That feeling alone can stop you from even starting. But each time you delete a picture that doesn't serve you, you make the task feel lighter and more achievable. Little by little, you create a space that feels organized and calm rather than chaotic.

Deleting also helps you see what you truly value. When you decide which pictures to remove, you're also deciding which ones matter most. That process of making choices can deepen your connection to the photos you keep. Rather than scrolling past dozens of nearly identical shots of the same sunset, you're left with the single image that takes your breath away every time you see it. In this way, deleting actually elevates your collection, turning it from a random assortment into a meaningful story.

For many people, the thought of deleting photos brings up fear. What if you regret it? What if you delete the wrong one? That hesitation is natural, but it doesn't have to stop you. There are ways to make deleting feel safer and more intentional. One simple method is to create a temporary "review" folder. As you go through your pictures, move any you're unsure about into this folder instead of deleting them outright. Give yourself a week or a month to think it over, then revisit and decide. Often, with fresh eyes, you'll find it easier to let go.

It can also help to establish a few clear rules for yourself before you start. For example, you might decide to delete any photo that is blurry or out of focus, duplicates where one is clearly better than the others, or pictures you don't even remember taking. You might also choose to delete screenshots of random things, photos of receipts, or anything you saved "just in case" but no longer need. Having guidelines like these gives you confidence as you sort.

Another advantage of deleting as you organize is that it saves you time later. Every extra photo you keep is another file you'll have to scroll past, back up, and possibly sort again in the future. By removing the unnecessary now, you're simplifying your life down the road. Your future self will thank you for the effort you put in today.

It's also worth thinking about how deleting makes sharing your collection easier. When you show friends and family your pictures, you don't want them sitting through a slideshow full of blurry shots, repeats, or pictures that mean nothing to them. A thoughtfully edited collection allows you to tell a clear, engaging story, one that holds their attention and makes them smile.

Even from a practical standpoint, deleting has benefits. Digital storage may feel unlimited, but it isn't truly free. Cloud services often charge more as your library grows, and large collections can slow down devices or take longer to back up. Deleting helps keep everything running smoothly and can even save you money if you avoid needing to upgrade to a larger plan unnecessarily.

For many people, the biggest hurdle to deleting is simply making the time for it. The idea of sorting through thousands of photos at once can feel intimidating. That's why it's helpful to tackle it in small, manageable chunks. You might decide to delete for just ten minutes a day, or focus on one folder or one event at a time. Breaking it down this way makes it less daunting and more likely to actually happen.

If you find yourself hesitating, try reminding yourself of the purpose of your collection. Your photos are meant to bring joy and preserve memories, not to overwhelm you. Each picture you delete is a step toward making your library a place you actually want to visit, full of moments that truly matter to you.

And remember, you're not erasing the memory itself when you delete a photo. You're simply choosing which version of the memory you want to hold onto. Keeping the one clear, beautiful shot of your grandson's birthday cake instead of ten slightly crooked or blurry ones doesn't diminish the day—it enhances it.

How to spot duplicates

It's surprisingly easy to end up with duplicate photos. With just a few swipes or taps, the same picture can quietly multiply across your devices, hiding in different folders, cloud backups, and memory cards. It doesn't take long before those doubles, triples, and even quadruples start cluttering your collection and making it harder to enjoy your best moments. Learning how to spot duplicates — and how to deal with them — is a skill that will save you time, space, and a lot of frustration.

One reason duplicates are tricky is that they aren't always exact copies in the way you might expect. A picture taken in burst mode, for example, can create five nearly identical shots in a single second. A photo downloaded from an email might sit side-by-side with the original already in your gallery. Even editing a picture — cropping, brightening, adding a filter — often leaves both the edited and original version behind. While it may not seem like much at first, over time these extra files pile up and make finding the one you want more challenging.

The first step in spotting duplicates is knowing where to look. Most of them hide in plain sight. Start by scrolling slowly through your photos on one device. You'll notice patterns emerge. Birthdays with fifteen nearly identical group shots. Vacations with row after row of the same sunset. Screenshots of a recipe saved three different times in a week.

As you move through, pay attention to photos that seem to tell the same story multiple times. You don't need all of them.

Once you've identified likely duplicates, the next step is to compare them closely. Often, two photos will look almost the same until you really study them. Look for small differences — is one slightly sharper? Are the colors more vibrant? Does one have everyone's eyes open while the other doesn't? You can then keep the version you feel best represents the memory and delete the others. Don't be afraid to zoom in and take your time. Choosing the better photo is part of crafting a collection you'll actually want to revisit.

Some people find it helpful to create a temporary "review" folder as they work. If you're unsure which version to keep, move both into the folder for now. Later, after a break, you can come back with fresh eyes and make your choice. This approach removes the pressure to decide everything at once and makes the process feel less daunting.

Another place duplicates often hide is between devices. A picture taken on your phone and later transferred to your computer might appear twice if both devices are backing up to the cloud. Similarly, if you email photos to yourself or download them from a text message without deleting the original, you can end up with copies. To address this, take a moment to check your photo libraries on each device and see if the same image is living in more than one place unnecessarily.

Many phones now have a built-in feature to help with

this. For example, some iPhones include a "Duplicates" album in the Photos app, where the phone automatically identifies images that appear to be the same and lets you merge them. It's worth exploring this feature if your device offers it — just remember to review before you merge, in case there's a subtle difference you want to keep.

On computers, spotting duplicates manually can be more of a challenge. Sorting your photos by date is a helpful start. When sorted this way, duplicates tend to line up next to each other, making them easier to compare. You can also sort by file name or size, which sometimes brings obvious duplicates together. Take your time, and don't rush through — this is a task where patience pays off.

If you're working with a particularly large collection and prefer a little assistance, there are tools that can help. Programs like Gemini, Duplicate Cleaner, and others are designed specifically to scan your folders and highlight files that look alike. These tools can save you hours, especially if your collection has grown over many years and you don't know where to begin. Just keep in mind that software isn't perfect — always review its recommendations before deleting anything.

It's also worth thinking about duplicates that aren't technically identical but still clutter your collection. For example, if you took a dozen shots of the same moment hoping to get the perfect one, and now you're left with all twelve, that's more than you need. Even if the camera saved each file with a slightly different name, they serve the same purpose. Go ahead and choose the single image you love most and let the others go.

Some duplicates are harder to let go of because they feel tied to a memory. You might hesitate, wondering if deleting a photo means erasing part of the moment. But keeping multiple blurry or awkward versions doesn't make the memory any stronger — in fact, it can drown out the one image that really does it justice. By narrowing down, you make your collection more meaningful.

One helpful mindset is to think of yourself as a curator rather than just a collector. A collector gathers everything, but a curator chooses what best represents the story. When you spot duplicates and decide which one tells the story better, you're acting as the curator of your own life. And that's a powerful feeling.

How to delete safely

There's something about pressing a delete button that can feel unsettling. Even when you're looking at a blurry photo or a picture of your feet that you didn't mean to take, a small voice whispers: what if I need that later? That feeling is perfectly normal, but it doesn't have to stop you from cleaning up your photo library. When done carefully and thoughtfully, deleting photos is one of the most important steps you can take to simplify your collection and enjoy it more. The key is to do it in a way that feels safe and gives you confidence.

A good place to start is by understanding what happens when you delete a photo. On most smartphones, computers, and even cloud services, deleting doesn't usually mean the photo disappears instantly and forever. Instead, it's moved to a "Recently Deleted" or "Trash" folder for a period of time—often thirty days. This acts as a safety net. If you realize you made a mistake or change your mind, you can restore the photo easily within that window. Knowing that takes some of the pressure off, and you can work without fear of making an irreversible choice.

When you're ready to start deleting, it helps to approach it in small batches. Trying to tackle thousands of photos at once can feel overwhelming and lead to mistakes. Focus on one folder, one event, or even just one year at a time. Move slowly through each set of pictures, and don't rush your decisions. You don't need to finish everything in one sitting. Even ten minutes a day adds up quickly to real progress.

As you scroll through your photos, keep a few simple guidelines in mind. Blurry pictures, accidental screenshots, duplicate versions of the same moment, and images that mean nothing to you are all good candidates for deletion. If you pause at a photo and feel unsure, skip it for now and come back later. There's no harm in leaving some for a second pass. Over time, you may find it easier to make decisions once you've built up some confidence.

On many devices, you can select multiple photos at once instead of deleting them one by one. This can save a lot of time. For example, you might highlight all the blurry pictures from one event and delete them in a single tap. The same goes for a series of nearly identical sunset shots or a long string of accidental selfies. Working in groups rather than individually makes the process less tedious.

One smart habit is to keep a backup before you start deleting in earnest. That way, you know there's still a full copy of your collection somewhere safe if you ever need it. You can use an external hard drive or a cloud backup service for this purpose. Think of it as your "just in case" copy. With that peace of mind, you'll find it easier to be decisive.

For those who are extra cautious, creating a temporary folder labeled something like "To Review" or "Maybe Delete" can be helpful. Instead of sending questionable photos straight to the trash, move them into this folder first. Let them sit there for a week or two. When you come back, you'll probably find it much easier to say goodbye to most of them.

Pay attention to how your devices and services handle deleted photos. On an iPhone, for example, you'll find a "Recently Deleted" album in the Photos app where deleted pictures remain for thirty days before being removed permanently. You can go into that folder and either recover or permanently delete photos whenever you like. Google Photos and other cloud services often have similar features. It's worth checking your settings and getting familiar with how long deleted items are kept before being erased for good.

Another consideration is deleting across multiple devices. If your phone, tablet, and computer are all syncing through a cloud service, deleting a photo on one device may remove it from all of them. That's usually the goal, but it can catch some people off guard. Before you begin, make sure you understand how your accounts are connected. If you prefer to delete photos only from a specific device while keeping the originals elsewhere, you may need to adjust your settings to prevent automatic syncing.

If you're cleaning up photos on a computer, one tip is to sort your files by date or name first. This helps bring duplicates and similar images together, making it easier to spot which ones can go. Many computers also let you preview images quickly without opening them fully, which can speed things up. If you're not sure about a file, you can always drag it to a temporary folder before deleting it completely.

It's also a good idea to check cloud services periodically to remove old or unwanted files. While it may feel like there's infinite space, many services charge more as your collection grows. Deleting unwanted photos helps keep your storage costs low and your library tidy.

Making decisions

One of the biggest challenges in organizing your digital photos is figuring out which ones deserve a place in your collection. Every picture represents a moment, but not every moment needs to live on in your library. Learning to make these decisions can feel daunting at first, but it's also one of the most rewarding parts of the process. When you finish, you're left with a set of photos that truly tell your story — one you can enjoy without distraction.

Begin by asking yourself what you want your photo library to say about your life. It doesn't need to include every single thing you've ever seen or done. Instead, think of it as a highlight reel — something that brings you joy when you look through it, and that others can enjoy with you. Keeping that bigger purpose in mind helps guide each choice.

When you start reviewing your photos, it helps to focus on the obvious ones first. Blurry shots, accidental pocket photos, and images where the subject is completely obscured can usually go without much thought. The same goes for multiples of the same scene. If you took ten pictures of your dog in the same pose, keep the one that makes you smile most and delete the rest. There's no benefit to keeping every version when one captures the feeling perfectly.

Another helpful approach is to look at each photo and notice how you feel when you see it. If it brings up a memory you treasure, or simply makes you happy, it's probably worth keeping. If it leaves you confused — "Why did I even take that?" — or reminds you of something unpleasant, you're better off letting it go. Trust that you don't need to hold on to every single frame to keep the memory alive.

Sometimes you'll come across a photo that you feel lukewarm about. It's not bad, but it's not great either. In those cases, it can be useful to compare it to others from the same event or day. Is there another photo that captures the moment better? If yes, then you've found your keeper, and the lesser one can be deleted. It's also perfectly fine to set these "maybe" photos aside in a temporary folder if you're not ready to decide yet. Giving yourself time to think often makes the decision easier later on.

Family events and group pictures can also be tricky. It's tempting to keep every single shot from holidays, weddings, and reunions, especially when other people are involved. But even here, you can still choose the ones that best tell the story. You don't need five slightly different pictures of everyone around the dinner table. One or two that show everyone at their best will mean more and be easier to share with others. The same is true for scenic shots. A single photo of the sunset or the view from your trip can bring the memory back just as well as a dozen nearly identical ones.

Another factor to consider is your audience. Are these photos just for you, or do you plan to share them with others? If you're putting together albums or slideshows for family, it's worth thinking about which images will resonate most with them. You may have a special fondness for that blurry snapshot of your kitchen remodel halfway through, but it's unlikely anyone else will miss it if you let it go. Choosing the best moments not only keeps your library tidy, it also makes it more meaningful for the people you share it with.

You may also want to think about the future. Over the years, your photo library can grow into an heirloom of sorts — something you pass down to children, grandchildren, or close friends. Keeping only the photos that truly matter ensures they inherit a collection that tells your story clearly and beautifully. It's easy to get lost in an endless scroll of similar, forgettable images. A curated collection gives your loved ones something they can enjoy without feeling overwhelmed.

Some people find it helpful to set simple rules for themselves. For example: keep only the best two or three pictures from any single event, delete any photo you don't recognize or understand, and limit yourself to one or two versions of any scene. Having clear guidelines helps take the emotion out of the process and speeds up decision-making.

If you're still finding it hard to let go, it can help to remind yourself that deleting a photo doesn't erase the memory itself. You still carry that moment with you. And, in most cases, you've likely kept at least one photo that preserves it. Letting go of extras is about giving the best memories room to shine. In fact, by reducing the clutter, you'll find you actually spend more time looking at and enjoying the photos you keep.

For the more sentimental among us, letting go can take practice. It may feel difficult at first, but it gets easier. Each time you delete a photo that doesn't serve your story, you're creating space for the ones that do. That act of selection makes your library feel more alive and personal. It becomes something you want to look through, instead of something you avoid because it feels too crowded or confusing.

6

CREATING FOLDERS & ALBUMS

One of the simplest ways to make your photo collection feel more manageable is to give it some structure. Right now, you might have all your photos jumbled together in one big pile on your phone or computer. Even if you've already deleted the obvious clutter and decided what to keep, scrolling endlessly through thousands of images can still feel like searching for a needle in a haystack. That's where folders and albums come in.

Creating folders and albums is like putting your photos into labeled boxes on a shelf. You always know where to look when you want something specific, and you spend much less time hunting around. Instead of relying on memory and endless scrolling, you can head straight to the section you need and enjoy your pictures right away.

Start by thinking about how you naturally remember your photos. Do you think of them by year? By event? By the people in them? By location? This can help you decide the best way to organize your folders. Some people like to set up a folder for each year and then add subfolders for holidays, birthdays, trips, or other special occasions. Others prefer to create folders named for the people or pets that appear in them most. There's no single right way — what matters is that it makes sense to you.

One big benefit of folders is that they help reduce the mental load of sorting through a massive library. Looking at a folder labeled "Hawaii 2018" or "Grandkids' Birthdays" is much less intimidating than scrolling through an endless grid of thumbnails trying to pick them out. Even if each folder holds dozens or hundreds of pictures, just having them gathered in one place is a big relief.

On many phones and computers, albums serve a similar purpose, though they work slightly differently. Albums don't move or duplicate your photos. Instead, they act like playlists for your pictures — you can create an album and add photos to it without removing them from your main library. This is handy if you want to group pictures in more than one way. For example, you might create an album of "Best of 2022" even though those same pictures also live in your "Family" or "Vacations" folders.

Albums can also help you create more focused collections to share with others. It's much nicer to show someone a short, organized album than to hand them your phone and let them scroll through everything. If you know you're going to a family gathering, you can put together an album of highlights from the past year and have it ready to show or even display as a slideshow.

Once you've decided on your folder or album system, the next step is to put it into action. Begin with a few simple categories rather than trying to perfect everything at once. You can always refine your system later as you get more comfortable. It's often helpful to start with your most recent photos, since those are fresh in your memory and more likely to be shared soon.

For older photos, take your time. Work in small batches — maybe one year or one big event at a time. You don't need to finish it all in one sitting. Even creating just a few folders to start with will make your library feel much more manageable.

Using folders and albums also has the benefit of making your backups cleaner and more useful. When you back up your photos to an external drive or cloud service, the folder structure often comes along with it. That means if you ever lose your device or need to restore your collection, you won't be left with a giant mess of unlabeled files. Instead, your organized system will still be there, ready for you to use.

Some devices even allow you to search within your

folders and albums. If you're looking for a specific event, typing the name of a folder — "Christmas" or "Beach Trip" — can bring it up instantly. This is a small feature, but it saves a lot of time and makes it more enjoyable to revisit your memories whenever you like.

If you're unsure whether to use folders, albums, or both, keep in mind that they can work together. On your computer, folders are often the best way to organize your actual files. On your phone or in a cloud service, albums are more flexible and allow you to group photos in ways that make sense for sharing or quick viewing. Many people find a combination works best — folders for permanent structure and albums for temporary or thematic groupings.

Suggested ways to organize

Once you've made the decision to organize your digital photos, the next question is how to actually arrange them in a way that works for you. There are many ways to do it, and the good news is there's no single right answer. The method you choose should reflect how you think about your own memories and what makes them easiest to find when you want to look back or share with others.

A great starting point is to organize by year. This method works well for nearly everyone because our lives already tend to be marked by years. Birthdays, holidays, trips, and milestones all fit naturally into a timeline. Creating folders or albums labeled with the year — "2020," "2021," "2022" — gives your collection a clear and simple backbone. From there, you can even create subfolders within each year for specific events or people if you want to get more detailed. This structure also makes it easy to keep up in the future, since every new set of photos simply goes into the current year's folder.

Another popular way to organize is by event. This approach is especially satisfying if you tend to take a lot of photos at specific occasions. Weddings, graduations, anniversaries, vacations, family reunions — these are the kinds of moments that stand out when you're reminiscing. You can create folders or albums named for the event, such as "Hawaii Trip 2017" or "Sam's 80th Birthday." The benefit of this method is that each group of photos tells a complete story, and you can jump right to the experience you're thinking of without having to sift through unrelated pictures.

Some people prefer to organize by person. This is particularly useful if you take a lot of pictures of your children, grandchildren, friends, or even pets. Creating albums labeled with names — "Emma," "Lucas," "Buddy the Dog" — helps you see all of someone's moments together in one place. It's a wonderful way to watch someone grow or relive shared memories. On many modern devices, facial recognition features can even help you identify and group photos of the same person automatically, which can save a lot of time.

Organizing by place is another option, especially if you

travel often or enjoy capturing landscapes. Creating folders or albums named for locations — "Paris," "Grand Canyon," "Lake House" — helps you collect all your photos from a particular spot, no matter when you were there. This method is especially satisfying for people who love seeing how places change over time or who enjoy looking back on adventures from different stages of life.

You don't have to choose just one method. Many people find a combination works best. For example, you could create main folders for each year, and then create albums within those years based on events or people. Or you might use folders for years and albums for favorite places or individual family members. The key is to find a system that makes sense to you and feels natural when you're looking for something.

It's worth taking a little time to think about which kind of organization matches the way your mind works. If you tend to think chronologically, organizing by year may feel the most comfortable. If your memories are tied more to milestones or special gatherings, organizing by event might fit better. If your focus is on loved ones, organizing by person can bring joy each time you open an album. And if you're someone who feels connected to the places you've been, organizing by location might be the most meaningful.

Keep in mind that whatever method you choose doesn't have to be permanent. As you work through your library, you may discover a preference you hadn't expected. You might start out organizing by year but find you enjoy grouping by event more. Or you might begin by creating folders for places and realize that adding albums for individual people brings your collection to life.

If you're not sure where to begin, pick the simplest option first. Organizing by year provides a natural structure that's easy to build on. Once you've created those basic folders, you can start creating additional albums or subfolders within them as you see patterns emerge.

Whichever approach you take, give yourself permission to adjust as you go. The process of organizing your photos is as much about learning what matters to you as it is about the technical details. The clearer your priorities become, the easier it is to choose a system that works.

One helpful tip is to use clear, specific names for your folders and albums. Instead of naming something "Vacation," use "Italy 2019" or "Florida Beach Trip." Instead of just "Birthday," try "Emma's 10th Birthday 2021." These details make it much easier to find what you're looking for later, especially as your collection grows.

How to rename files so they make sense

A big part of keeping your photos organized is making sure each file has a name that actually tells you what it is. By default, most cameras, smartphones, and even computers give your pictures names that don't mean anything to you. You've probably seen files with names like "IMG_0456.JPG" or "DSC100034.PNG." When you only have a handful of photos, this isn't such a problem. But when you're trying to sort through hundreds—or even thousands—it becomes clear very quickly how confusing it can get. Giving your photos meaningful names turns your collection from a jumble of random codes into something you can navigate and enjoy.

Think of your file names like labels on boxes. A box labeled "Memories" isn't much help when you're looking for something specific, but a box labeled "Hawaii Trip 2019 - Sunset Beach" tells you exactly what you'll find inside. Your digital photos deserve the same kind of care.

You don't have to rename every single photo individually to make progress. Start by thinking about how you already decided to organize your folders or albums. If you've chosen to organize by year and event, then your file names can follow a similar structure. A good file name often has three key pieces of information: date, event or subject, and an optional detail.

For example, instead of keeping a photo called "IMG_1234.JPG," you might rename it to something like "2021-12-25_Christmas_Morning_GiftOpening.JPG." Even if you don't remember every detail just by glancing at the photo, the file name gives you clues about where it belongs and what it represents.

Some people prefer to keep it even simpler. You could just use "2021-12-25_Christmas1.JPG," "2021-12-25_Christmas2.JPG," and so on. Others include names if the photo focuses on a person: "2022-06-15_Grandkids_Emma_Lucas.JPG." There's no rule here, other than making sure the names are clear and consistent.

It helps to choose a pattern and stick with it. For dates, writing them in year-month-day order (YYYY-MM-DD) is a good habit because it keeps everything in chronological order when sorted alphabetically. This way, all your 2021 pictures will group together automatically, followed by 2022, and so on.

If you're not sure where to start, try this basic pattern:

Year-Month-Day_EventOrSubject_OptionalDetail.JPG

Here are a few more examples of helpful names:

- 2019-07-04_IndependenceDay_Fireworks.JPG
- 2020-11-26_Thanksgiving_DinnerTable.JPG
- 2021-03-15_Lucas_BirthdayCake.JPG

- 2022-08-12_Vacation_Yellowstone_Bison.JPG

THIS DOESN'T MEAN you have to type out every single name manually. On computers, there are ways to rename multiple files at once. This is called "batch renaming," and it's a lifesaver when you have dozens of pictures from one event. For example, you can select all the photos from your 2022 Thanksgiving dinner, rename the first one to "2022-11-24_Thanksgiving_1," and your computer will automatically rename the others with "_2," "_3," and so on. Different systems have slightly different ways to do this, but the concept is the same: you only need to type the name once, and the rest will follow your pattern.

Taking the time to rename your files also makes it easier to back them up and restore them later. If you ever have to recover photos from a backup or share them with family, meaningful file names ensure everyone knows what's what. It also makes it easier to search for specific photos using the search bar on your computer, phone, or cloud service. Instead of scrolling through hundreds of thumbnails, you can type in "Birthday" or "Hawaii" and find what you need instantly.

If you're overwhelmed by the thought of renaming thousands of photos, you don't have to tackle it all at once. Start with your most important folders — maybe the last two or three years of holidays and milestones. Or even just pick one big trip or family event and work through those. Every little bit you do improves your collection, and you can always come back to it later.

It's also okay to leave casual or everyday snapshots unnamed if you're not sure yet what to call them. Focus on the photos that matter most and that you're likely to revisit or share. Those are the ones that benefit most from clear, descriptive names.

Some people like to add little notes into their file names, too. Things like "best" or "print" or "slideshow" can help you remember which pictures stood out. For example: "2021-12-25_Christmas_Morning_Best.JPG." This makes it easy to spot your favorites when you're putting together albums or gifts later.

The main thing to remember is that your file names should make sense to you. They don't have to be perfect or fancy. They just need to help you recognize the photo without opening it. Once you've gotten into the habit of renaming as you go, it becomes second nature. Over time, your library becomes something you can actually use and enjoy instead of something you avoid because it feels too messy.

How to create albums on your phone and on your computer

Giving your photos clear names is an excellent way to make your collection more manageable. Once you've done that, you can take things a step further by grouping your pictures into albums. Albums add another layer of order to your library and make it much easier to enjoy your best moments without digging through everything else. Albums also make sharing simpler, whether you're showing someone your last vacation or sending a grandchild a slideshow of their childhood highlights. Learning how to create albums on your phone and on your computer can save you time and make your digital life feel more organized and intentional.

On your phone, creating albums is straightforward. Both iPhones and Android phones include a built-in photo app that makes it easy to group pictures. On an iPhone, open the Photos app and tap on the "Albums" tab at the bottom. There you'll see a plus sign (+) or an option called "New Album." Tap it, give your album a name that makes sense to you — like "Spring Break 2023" or "Family Birthdays" — and press save. Then you can scroll through your photo library, select the images you want, and add them to that album. The originals stay in your main photo library, but the album acts like a curated playlist, gathering only the pictures you want to see together. Android works much the same way, though sometimes it calls them

"Folders" or "Collections" depending on your model or software. Look for the menu options in your Photos or Gallery app and follow the prompts to create a new album.

Albums on your phone are especially handy because you carry your phone with you everywhere. When someone asks to see pictures of a specific event or person, you can go straight to the right album instead of swiping endlessly through unrelated shots. It also means you're less likely to skip over old favorites simply because they're buried under newer photos. Some phones even let you create "Shared Albums" — which are private albums you can share with specific friends or family members who can view and even add their own photos to the collection. This is a thoughtful way to keep everyone connected after a family trip, holiday, or special gathering.

On your computer, the principle is the same, though the process looks a little different. If you use a Windows computer, the built-in Photos app lets you create albums in a similar way. Open the app, find the "Albums" section, and select "New Album." From there, you can name the album and add photos by browsing your folders or letting the app suggest groupings based on dates and faces. On a Mac, the Photos app offers the same convenience. You can create albums by selecting your pictures, then choosing "File" and "New Album," or by right-clicking and selecting the album option. You can even create "Smart Albums," which automatically update to include photos that match certain criteria, like every photo tagged with a certain person's name.

One of the advantages of creating albums on your computer is that you can often work with a bigger screen and more tools. You can sort by date, drag and drop to rearrange pictures, and even make small edits as you organize. Albums created on your computer also sync with many cloud services, so the same albums show up on your phone if you're logged into the same account.

Albums are also a powerful way to prepare photos for projects, such as slideshows, printed books, or gifts. If you're planning to make a printed photo book for someone's birthday, you can gather all the relevant pictures into a single album before you upload them to a printing service. Or you can create a holiday slideshow album that automatically plays in order without interruptions from unrelated pictures. Having everything grouped ahead of time keeps the process simple and stress-free.

As you build your albums, don't worry about getting everything perfect right away. Start with a few obvious groupings — big trips, holidays, milestones — and then add more as you work through your library. You can always move pictures between albums later. Many apps even let you put the same picture in more than one album. A single photo of your granddaughter blowing out birthday candles could appear in both a "Birthdays" album and a "Grandkids" album. That flexibility is one of the great benefits of using albums rather than moving files into separate folders.

If you'd like, you can even experiment with themes. Some people create albums called "Best of the Year," where they collect their favorite photos from a given year. Others make albums based on moods or colors, like "Sunsets" or "Black & White Favorites." You can be as creative or as practical as you like. The point is to make it easier to enjoy and share your pictures, not to create an elaborate system you won't stick with.

7

BACKING UP YOUR MEMORIES

There's a certain peace of mind that comes from knowing your memories are safe. That peace is what backing up your photos gives you. Once you've put in the effort to sort, name, and organize your pictures into meaningful albums, the last thing you want is to lose all of it because of something unexpected. Backing up isn't just a technical step—it's a way to protect the time, care, and emotion you've invested in your photo collection.

It helps to think of your photos as something more than just digital files. Every one of them represents a moment you can't repeat. A first birthday, a quiet afternoon in the garden, a family reunion, a trip to the mountains. These moments deserve a little extra attention because they carry your history. And the truth is, technology isn't perfect. Phones get dropped, computers crash, hard drives wear out, and even cloud services can have hiccups. It's not a matter of if a device will fail, but when. That's why it's so important to make sure your photos are saved somewhere else—preferably more than one somewhere else.

Backing up doesn't have to be complicated. It can be as simple as copying your photos onto an external hard drive, uploading them to a cloud service, or both. The key is redundancy—having your pictures in more than one place. If your computer dies tomorrow, you should still be able to access your photos somewhere else. If your phone gets lost on a trip, you shouldn't have to say goodbye to years of memories.

One of the biggest misconceptions about digital photos is that they're "safe" just because they're digital. People often assume that if a photo isn't on paper, it can't get ruined. But digital photos are just as vulnerable, in their own way. They can get corrupted if a file becomes damaged. They can disappear if you accidentally press the wrong button. And storage devices, just like any other equipment, don't last forever. That's why backing up isn't optional—it's essential.

There's also the emotional cost of not backing up. Losing a device might mean more than just losing some money. It can feel like losing part of your life. Many people have stories of phones falling into pools or computers breaking down, only to realize too late that nothing was saved elsewhere. The regret is sharp because it's often avoidable.

If you're already in the habit of creating albums, backing up fits right into that routine. Once you've put together an album of last year's holidays or a grandchild's graduation, you can back up that album in just a few clicks. And the best part is that backups don't have to take much time once the initial setup is done. Many services and devices even let you schedule automatic backups, which means you don't have to remember to do it every week or month. It just happens in the background while you go about your day.

Backing up also gives you freedom. Once you know your pictures are safe, you can feel more comfortable deleting unnecessary duplicates from your phone or camera to free up space. You don't have to keep everything cluttered on one device just because you're afraid to lose it. This makes it easier to maintain your collection and keep things tidy.

It's worth mentioning that backing up also makes sharing simpler. If you're keeping your photos only on your phone, it can be a chore to send pictures to family or create slideshows. But if your pictures are also stored on your computer and a cloud service, you can access them from wherever you are and share them with just a link or a few clicks. That accessibility is a wonderful side benefit of having your collection backed up properly.

Some people feel intimidated by the idea of setting up backups because they think it's something only "techies" can handle. But today's tools are designed to be friendly and easy.

An external hard drive, for example, plugs into your computer and often comes with simple software that walks you through the process. Many cloud services like Google Photos, iCloud, or Amazon Photos even offer apps that handle the backups automatically once you sign in. You don't need to understand all the details about how it works; you just need to follow a few prompts, and your pictures are protected.

You might also be wondering how many backups you really need. At minimum, it's a good idea to have two copies: one local (like on your computer or external drive) and one offsite (like in the cloud). This way, you're protected both from a device failure and from something unexpected, like fire or theft at home. Having two backups might sound excessive at first, but when you consider how irreplaceable your photos are, it feels more like common sense.

How to back up to an external hard drive

Once you understand why it's so important to back up your photos, the next step is to actually do it. One of the easiest and most reliable ways to create a backup is by using an external hard drive. These small, portable devices give you a safe place to store your pictures outside of your computer or phone, and they're simple enough that anyone can use them without much technical know-how. Even if you've never held an external hard drive before, you can learn to use one with just a little guidance.

An external hard drive is about the size of a paperback book and plugs into your computer using a USB cable. You can find them at any electronics store or online, and they come in different sizes—measured in terabytes, which is just a fancy way of saying "a whole lot of space." Even a modestly sized drive has enough room for thousands and thousands of photos. When you pick one out, look for something described as "plug-and-play" or "compatible with your operating system," which just means it's designed to work right out of the box on your type of computer.

When you're ready to begin, clear a little space on your desk, set the external hard drive next to your computer, and connect the two with the included cable. On most computers, a window will pop up automatically letting you know that the drive has been detected. You might see it labeled as something like "External Drive" or the brand name of the device. On a Windows computer, it shows up in File Explorer as a new drive letter. On a Mac, it appears on the desktop or in Finder.

Before you copy anything over, it's a good idea to make a folder on your external hard drive just for your photos. You can name it something simple like "Photo Backup" or even include the year if you're backing up a particular set, such as "Photo Backup 2023." Creating folders on the drive works the same way as creating folders on your computer—right-click, select "New Folder," and type a name.

Now comes the part that feels rewarding: moving your photos. Open the folder on your computer where your photos are stored, and open the folder on the external drive side by side. Then, drag and drop the files or folders you want to back up into the new folder on your external drive. You can select entire folders at once, or pick specific albums you've already organized. The computer will start copying them over, and you'll see a progress bar letting you know how long it will take. Depending on how many pictures you have, this can take a few minutes or more. Just let it finish and avoid disconnecting the drive until the transfer is complete.

One of the advantages of backing up this way is that your photos remain in their original format, exactly as you organized them. This means that if anything happens to your main computer, you can just plug the external hard drive into another machine and still have access to all your files. It's also portable, which makes it easy to take with you if you're visiting family or moving between locations.

Once the copying is finished, double-check your external drive to make sure everything you intended to back up is actually there. Open a few folders and view a few pictures. This step takes only a minute or two but ensures your efforts paid off. Then, properly "eject" the drive before you unplug it —on Windows you can right-click and select "Eject," and on a Mac you drag the drive icon to the trash. This protects your files from getting corrupted.

If you're backing up a large collection, it can help to make a habit of doing it regularly rather than waiting until your photos pile up again. You can even add a note on your calendar once a month or once a quarter to remind yourself. Each time you back up, you can either replace the older files completely, or create new folders labeled by date, like "Backup July 2023" and "Backup October 2023." Keeping a few older copies can be handy in case you need to retrieve something you deleted months ago.

Some external drives come with their own software to automate this process. When you first plug in the drive, it might prompt you to install a program that can schedule automatic backups. If you feel comfortable following the instructions, this can save you time down the road, as the software will remember what you've already backed up and only copy new or changed files. But if you'd rather keep things simple, manual drag-and-drop works just as well.

It's also wise to store the external hard drive somewhere safe when you're not using it. Keeping it in a drawer, on a shelf, or even in a small fireproof box is better than leaving it out where it could get bumped or damaged. Since it's separate from your computer, it serves as a reliable backup even if your computer stops working.

How to back up to the cloud

For many people, the idea of "the cloud" can feel a little mysterious at first. It's not something you can hold in your hand like an external hard drive, and it doesn't live in your home where you can see it. Yet it's become one of the most popular ways to keep photos safe and accessible. Backing up your photos to the cloud is one of the smartest habits you can develop, and it can be surprisingly simple once you understand how it works and what steps to take.

At its heart, the cloud is just a secure storage space provided by a company that you can access through the internet. Instead of keeping your photos only on your computer or phone, you send copies to this online storage space. The company's computers—called servers—hold your files safely and make them available to you whenever you need them. You can log in and see your photos from any device with an internet connection, whether it's your laptop, tablet, phone, or even a public computer while traveling.

One of the big advantages of cloud backup is that you don't have to worry about losing a physical device. If your phone is stolen or your computer breaks, your photos are still there, waiting for you in your cloud account. It's a modern way of making sure your memories are always within reach, even if the technology you're using today is no longer around tomorrow.

To start, you'll need to choose a cloud service. Many

people already have one available without realizing it. If you use an iPhone, Apple iCloud is built in. If you use an Android phone or have a Gmail account, Google Photos is already part of your account. Amazon also offers Amazon Photos as part of its Prime membership, and there are other options like Dropbox and Microsoft OneDrive. All of these services are designed to be user-friendly and guide you through the process step by step.

Once you've chosen a service, the next step is creating an account if you don't already have one. That usually just means entering your name, email address, and creating a password. If you already use the service for email or shopping, you may already have an account you can use.

From there, you install the app or program on the device where your photos are stored. On your phone, that might mean downloading the Google Photos app or making sure iCloud is turned on in your settings. On your computer, you can log in to the service through your web browser or download their desktop app.

When you open the app, it will typically ask you if you'd like to back up your photos. Say yes, and it will begin scanning your device for pictures. Depending on how many you have and how fast your internet connection is, this first backup can take anywhere from a few minutes to a few hours. The nice thing is, you don't have to sit there and watch it. You can go about your day, and the app will quietly work in the background.

Some services give you the option to back up only certain folders, or to include videos as well as photos. You can also choose whether to back up full-resolution versions of your photos or slightly smaller ones to save space. If you're not sure, full-resolution is the better choice because it preserves the highest quality.

Once the initial backup is complete, the cloud service will usually keep track of your new photos automatically. Every time you take a new picture on your phone or transfer one to your computer, the app notices and uploads it for you. This automatic feature means you don't have to remember to back up every week or month—it just happens for you.

If you prefer to have more control over what gets backed up, you can also do it manually. On your computer, you can drag and drop photo folders into the cloud app or web page. On your phone, you can select specific albums or individual pictures to upload. Both options work just fine, and you can choose whichever approach feels more comfortable.

One helpful tip is to check your cloud account from time to time to make sure everything looks right. Log in, browse through your albums, and see that the photos you care about most are safely stored there. If you notice something missing, you can always add it manually.

Most cloud services give you a certain amount of free storage space. For example, Apple iCloud starts you off with 5 gigabytes, and Google Photos used to offer unlimited space for lower-resolution photos. These days, you'll likely need to pay a few dollars per month if you have a large collection. The fee is usually very modest and worth it for the peace of mind.

Another benefit of cloud backup is that it makes sharing much easier. Once your photos are in the cloud, you can send a link to family and friends instead of emailing large files. You can even create shared albums where everyone can add their own pictures from a family event or trip.

Some people worry about security when storing pictures online. It's a reasonable concern, but cloud services use strong encryption and other protections to keep your data private. You can also add extra security by choosing a strong password and enabling two-factor authentication, which just means the service will text you a code when you log in from a new device.

Cloud backup also pairs nicely with an external hard drive. One gives you local access at home, while the other ensures you're protected even if something happens to your home equipment. Many people feel most secure when they have both, and it doesn't take much more effort.

Setting up automatic backups

When you've worked hard to gather and organize your favorite pictures, it's only natural to want to protect them with as little effort as possible. While backing up your photos by hand is perfectly fine, there's an easier way that saves time and ensures you won't forget: automatic backups. Once you set them up, your devices will quietly do the work for you in the background, giving you one less thing to worry about.

Automatic backups work like a helpful assistant, constantly watching for new photos and making sure they're safely saved elsewhere. You don't need to remember which ones you've already backed up or sit down every week to move files yourself. For many people, this one simple change is what finally gives them peace of mind about their photo collection.

Most devices you already use—your smartphone, tablet, or computer—are designed to work with automatic backups. The key is turning on the right settings and knowing where your photos are being sent. Let's walk through the most common ways to make it happen.

On a smartphone, automatic backup is usually tied to your cloud service. If you use an iPhone, open the Settings app and tap your name at the top of the screen. From there, go to iCloud, then Photos, and make sure "iCloud Photos" is switched on. When this feature is enabled, your phone uploads every new photo you take to your iCloud account automatically. You can check that it's working by logging into iCloud.com on a computer and browsing your photos.

On an Android phone, the process is just as straightforward. Open the Google Photos app, tap your profile picture or initials in the top corner, and look for "Photos settings." Inside, you'll find "Backup & sync." Turn it on, and your phone will begin uploading every picture you take to your Google account. You can also check your storage here, and adjust whether the backup happens over Wi-Fi only or even when using mobile data.

If you prefer to back up to another cloud service, like Dropbox or Amazon Photos, download their app from your phone's app store and log in. Each one will walk you through turning on automatic photo upload, usually during the first setup. Once activated, they'll keep track of any new pictures you take without you having to lift a finger.

On your computer, you can also enable automatic backups. Many cloud services offer software you can install that monitors your chosen folders. For example, if you install Dropbox or OneDrive on your computer, you can point it at your "Pictures" folder. Every time you add new files to that folder, the software uploads them to your cloud account.

If you're more comfortable backing up to an external hard drive, you can still automate that process. On a Windows computer, the built-in "File History" feature can automatically copy your files to an external drive at regular intervals. You just plug in the drive, turn on File History in your system settings, and select which folders to back up. Windows will handle the rest from then on.

Mac computers have a similar feature called "Time Machine." Once you connect an external drive, your Mac will ask if you want to use it for backups. Agree, and it will start saving copies of your entire system—including your photos—hourly. Time Machine even keeps older versions of files, which can come in handy if you accidentally delete something.

Many external hard drives now come with their own backup software as well. When you first plug them in, they often offer to install a program that helps you schedule and customize your backups. Some even have a button you can press right on the drive to start a backup manually whenever you like.

No matter which option you choose, it's worth taking a few minutes to check the settings once your automatic backups are running. For cloud services, make sure they're set to upload in full resolution if you want to preserve the highest quality. Check your storage space from time to time so you're not surprised when it fills up. For external drives, keep them plugged in or connect them regularly if you want to stay up-to-date.

Some people like to set a specific time each week or month to double-check that everything's working. This is especially helpful if you don't leave your external drive connected all the time. Even with automatic systems, it's smart to be sure nothing has gone wrong—like a password that needs updating or a drive that wasn't plugged in.

If you find yourself traveling often or switching between devices, automatic backups become even more valuable. No matter where you are or which device you're using, your photos are kept current and safe. Even if you drop your phone on vacation or your laptop stops working at home, you'll still have everything backed up and waiting.

One of the best things about automatic backups is how they remove the mental load. Instead of worrying about when you last saved your photos or which ones you might have missed, you can simply enjoy taking pictures. The technology handles the rest quietly in the background.

8

SHARING YOUR PHOTOS

There are few things more satisfying than sharing a special photo with someone you care about. Whether it's a picture of a grandchild's birthday, a snapshot from a beautiful trip, or just a funny moment you happened to catch, being able to send it quickly by email is one of the simplest ways to stay connected. It's personal, instant, and feels thoughtful. Yet for many people, attaching and sending photos by email can feel a little intimidating the first few times. The good news is that once you understand the basic steps, it's just as easy as writing the message itself.

The first thing to keep in mind is that all email services—Gmail, Yahoo, Outlook, AOL, or others—work in roughly the same way when it comes to adding photos. They each have slightly different screens or wording, but they all include a button that allows you to attach a file to your message. That button is the key to sending photos.

Begin by logging into your email account on your computer, tablet, or phone. Once you're in your inbox, look for a button or link that says "Compose," "New Message," or simply has a pencil or plus sign icon. Click or tap it, and you'll see a blank message form appear, ready for you to fill in.

At the top of the message, you'll see spaces for the recipient's email address, the subject line, and the message body. In the "To" field, type the email address of the person you want to send the photo to. It's a good idea to double-check that address for typos, as one wrong letter can send your photo somewhere else or bounce back as undeliverable.

Next, write a subject line that helps the recipient know what they're about to open. Something as simple as "Photo from our family picnic" or "Birthday picture of Anna" works perfectly. Then, in the body of the message, you can add a little note if you like—maybe explaining when or where the photo was taken, or just saying hello.

Now it's time to attach the photo. On your screen, there should be a small icon that looks like a paperclip. That's the universal symbol for "attachment." Click or tap on it, and a new window will open showing the files on your device. From here, you'll need to navigate to where your photo is saved. If you're on your computer, it may be in your "Pictures" folder or on your desktop. If you're using your phone, you may see your camera roll or gallery pop up automatically.

Once you find the photo you want to send, click or tap on it, then click "Open" or "Choose." You'll see the file name appear in your email message, usually below the subject line or at the bottom of the message box. Some email services even show you a small preview of the picture. That's how you know it's attached and ready to go.

If you want to send more than one photo, you can repeat the process by clicking the paperclip icon again and selecting another file. Most email services let you attach several photos at once, but keep in mind that large numbers of high-resolution photos can make your message too big to send. If you see a warning about file size, you can try sending fewer photos at a time or resizing them to a smaller size.

Many smartphones and tablets actually offer a shortcut for emailing a photo directly from your photo gallery. On an iPhone, for example, open the Photos app, find and tap the picture you want, then tap the share icon (a square with an arrow pointing up). One of the options will be "Mail." Choose that, and your email app will open with the photo already attached and ready for you to address and send. Android phones have a similar process, usually involving the "Share" button and selecting your email app from the list of options.

Once your message is addressed, written, and the photo is attached, give it one last look to make sure everything looks right. Then click or tap the "Send" button. Depending on the size of the photo and the speed of your internet connection, it might take a few seconds for your message to leave your outbox. If you want to check that it was sent successfully, you can look in your "Sent" folder to see a copy of the message.

If you're sending to someone who checks email on their phone or tablet, it's a good idea to keep your photos at a reasonable size. Very large pictures can take longer to download and might use up their mobile data. Most devices and email services automatically adjust the size of attached photos, but if you're asked whether to send "small," "medium," or "large," choosing medium is usually a safe choice for sharing.

How to share on Facebook or other social media

Sharing photos on social media has become a way many families and friends stay connected. Whether it's showing a favorite vacation spot, celebrating a milestone, or just letting others see a slice of your day, posting pictures on Facebook or similar platforms helps others feel close to you. Even if you don't consider yourself someone who uses social media often, learning how to post photos can open the door to more conversations and bring kind comments from people you care about.

It helps to think of Facebook and other social media sites

as digital bulletin boards. When you post a photo, it's like pinning it to the board for your circle of friends to see. They can "like" it, leave a comment, or even share it further. You're still in control of what you show and who can see it, which is part of what makes it feel comfortable once you know your way around.

The first step is to log into your Facebook account on a computer, tablet, or phone. On the home screen, you'll see a box near the top that says something like "What's on your mind?" or "Write a post." That's where you start. Click or tap in that box, and it will open up into a larger window where you can type your message and attach your photo.

You'll see a little camera icon, a photo icon, or a button labeled "Photo/Video." Click or tap that, and your device will show you a list of files or your photo gallery. Find the picture you'd like to share, click or tap it, and you'll see it appear in your post. If you'd like, you can add a short caption above the photo, like "Beautiful sunset at the lake" or "Grandkids visiting today." Captions can help people understand what they're looking at, but they're not required.

Before you hit the "Post" button, it's worth checking who can see your photo. On Facebook, there's usually a little menu next to the "Post" button that says something like "Friends" or "Public." If you choose "Friends," only people you've added as friends on Facebook will be able to see it. If you choose "Public," anyone can see it. Many people feel more comfortable keeping their posts visible to friends only, and you can always change your mind later.

On other social media platforms, like Instagram, the process is very similar. Open the Instagram app, tap the plus sign at the bottom or top of the screen, and choose "Post." Your photo gallery will open, and you can select one or more pictures. Instagram also lets you add a short caption and even apply filters if you want to change the look of the picture. Then tap "Share," and it's posted to your profile for your followers to see.

One of the benefits of sharing photos this way is that people can react to them almost instantly. You might get comments from a cousin you haven't spoken to in months or a message from an old friend saying how much they enjoyed seeing your family. These little interactions can brighten your day and make the effort feel worthwhile.

If you'd rather not post publicly, many social media platforms also let you send a photo privately through their messaging features. On Facebook, for example, you can open Messenger, start a conversation with the person you want to share with, and tap the little photo icon to attach your picture. Only that person—or group—will see it.

Privacy is important, especially when sharing photos that feel more personal. If you're unsure about sharing something, it's okay to ask yourself whether you'd feel comfortable with anyone else seeing it. If the answer is no, it may be better to send it privately rather than post it for all your friends to view.

It's also a good idea to pay attention to how your photos are displayed once they're uploaded. Sometimes, Facebook or Instagram will crop your picture slightly or make it look smaller. You can adjust the crop by clicking or dragging it into position before posting. If your photo looks blurry or unclear, it could mean the original file was too small or low-quality. You can usually avoid that by uploading the full-sized version from your camera or phone rather than a screenshot.

Social media can be a wonderful way to create ongoing conversations around your photos. Many people find that when they share an old family picture, others chime in with memories, stories, and even additional photos they had forgotten. That sense of connection and shared history is one of the best parts of using these platforms.

If you're new to Facebook or any other social media, don't feel you have to post daily or even weekly. It's perfectly fine to use it only when you feel you have something worth sharing. People appreciate authenticity—pictures that feel real and meaningful are often more appreciated than dozens of random snapshots.

For those who prefer to avoid social media altogether but still want a similar experience, there are private photo-sharing services like Google Photos or private Facebook groups. These allow you to share albums or updates only with selected people, giving you control without missing out on connection.

Creating digital photo albums and slideshows

One of the most rewarding parts of organizing your photos is seeing them come to life in a way that others can enjoy, too. When you create a digital photo album or a slideshow, you're not just tidying up files—you're crafting a story. It becomes more than a collection of pictures. It's an experience your friends and family can follow and appreciate. And it can be a wonderful way for you to revisit meaningful moments without having to click through hundreds of disorganized images.

Albums and slideshows may sound like two different things, but they're really two sides of the same coin. A digital album is a set of photos grouped together, typically displayed in an online folder or gallery. A slideshow is simply an album presented one photo at a time, automatically moving through the pictures, often with transitions and music. Both can be created easily with tools already on your phone, tablet, or computer.

To start, think about what kind of album you want to make. It could be by event—like "Hawaii Trip 2021" or "Ella's High School Graduation." It might be by theme, such as "Family Pets" or "Gardens Through the Years." You can also organize by people or places. The most important thing is to pick something that has meaning to you, which will also make it more enjoyable to share.

If you're using your phone, the built-in Photos app already offers options for creating albums. On an iPhone, open the Photos app and go to the "Albums" tab. Tap the plus sign and select "New Album." You'll be asked to give it a name, and then you can select the photos you want to include. Once it's created, you can open that album anytime, and all the pictures you chose will be neatly displayed together. Android phones work similarly, though the wording may differ slightly. Look for "Create album" or "Add album" in your photo gallery app.

Tablets and computers usually offer more space and larger screens, which can make it easier to select and arrange your pictures. On a Windows computer, the Photos app lets you create albums by selecting your images, clicking the "New Album" button, and giving your collection a name. Macs offer the same in the Photos app—just select the photos and click the plus sign to create a new album.

Once you've created an album, you can rearrange the order of the photos if you like. Many apps let you drag pictures into place, helping you tell the story just the way you want. You might put your favorite shot at the beginning, group similar moments together, or end with a memorable closing image.

If you want to take it one step further and create a slideshow, most apps make it just as easy. On an iPhone or iPad, you can open an album and tap the three dots in the corner to find the "Slideshow" option. Your pictures will play one after another, complete with transitions and even music. On a Mac, there's a "Slideshow" button you can click, and it gives you choices of themes and songs. Windows computers also include slideshow features, usually in the Photos app or through PowerPoint if you'd like more creative control.

Slideshows are particularly nice for special occasions. For example, you might create one to play on a television screen during a birthday party or a family reunion. Many modern TVs let you connect a USB drive or even cast the slideshow from your phone or tablet directly to the screen. This can turn your photos into a centerpiece of the gathering, sparking stories and laughter as everyone watches together.

One of the joys of slideshows is that they feel more alive than scrolling through pictures. You don't have to do any clicking—just sit back and let the memories play. If you'd like, you can even add captions or titles to certain photos to explain what's happening or who is in the picture. Some apps let you record a short voice message or add background music that fits the mood of your album.

There are also free and paid websites that specialize in helping you create digital albums and slideshows. Sites like Google Photos, Shutterfly, and SmugMug let you upload your pictures, organize them, and then share a link to your album. These services often provide more creative templates and designs, which can make your presentation feel polished and professional. And because they live on the web, your friends and family can view them from anywhere, even if they don't have a social media account.

If you prefer to keep everything private, don't worry—most of these services let you control who can see your albums by sending invitations or links to specific people only.

Creating albums and slideshows can also help you feel less overwhelmed by the sheer number of photos you've collected. Rather than facing thousands of disorganized images, you can focus on curating just a few dozen at a time. This gives you a manageable goal, and over time you'll find your library feels much more under control.

One helpful habit is to create albums as you go. After a trip or event, take a few minutes to gather the best photos into an album right away. That way, you'll never have to dig through your entire gallery months later when you want to find them. And if you decide to make a slideshow, you'll already have the photos neatly grouped and ready to go.

Printing photo books and gifts online

There's something deeply satisfying about holding a photo in your hand. As much as digital albums and slideshows bring convenience and connection, a printed picture offers a kind of permanence and warmth that a glowing screen simply can't replicate. Many people find joy in taking their favorite digital images and turning them into beautiful, tangible keepsakes through photo books and personalized gifts. Doing this online is easier than you might think, and it can open up a whole new way to share your stories and celebrate your memories.

Photo books have become one of the most popular ways to preserve and showcase collections of pictures. They're essentially modern scrapbooks—sleek, sturdy books filled with your chosen photographs, printed on high-quality paper with professional binding. The beauty of a photo book is that it feels purposeful. Rather than scrolling endlessly through dozens of random snapshots, you can flip through pages that tell a clear and meaningful story.

Creating a photo book online starts with choosing a service. Well-known companies like Shutterfly, Snapfish, Mixbook, and even Costco offer websites designed to guide you through the process step by step. Most of these sites work similarly: you upload your photos, choose a layout and design, and arrange the pictures in the order you prefer. You can add captions, decorative backgrounds, and even themed embellishments if you like.

One of the first decisions you'll make is what kind of book you want. Many sites offer a variety of sizes, from small, square books perfect for a coffee table, to large, hardcover albums for weddings or family reunions. Some even have lay-flat pages, which allow your book to open completely flat without bending the middle of the photos—perfect for wide group shots or panoramic landscapes.

As you arrange your photos on each page, you'll often be given templates to choose from. These templates can help you make the most of your space, combining multiple pictures on a single page or highlighting one photo across an entire spread. If you feel creative, you can often move photos around freely, resize them, or change backgrounds and colors to fit your style.

One helpful feature many sites include is automatic placement. If sorting through dozens of photos feels daunting, the site can automatically arrange your pictures into the book for you. You can always go back and tweak it afterward, but it's a quick way to get started.

In addition to books, these same services offer an incredible variety of personalized photo gifts. Think beyond traditional prints and frames—your pictures can be printed on calendars, mugs, tote bags, blankets, and even puzzles. These gifts make thoughtful surprises for birthdays, holidays, or just to show someone you're thinking of them. A mug with your grandchild's face on it, a calendar featuring family photos through the year, or a soft throw blanket covered in favorite memories can bring a smile every time it's used.

One of the most practical and appreciated gifts is a custom calendar. Many people enjoy flipping through a calendar month by month and seeing a new family photo each time. You can choose themed designs, add notes or birthdays to specific dates, and make it uniquely personal to your family's story.

If you're worried about the technical side of uploading photos and placing orders, don't be. These websites are designed to be user-friendly, with clear instructions and previews at every step. Most have support options like live chat or customer service phone numbers in case you get stuck. Many also let you save your project and come back to it later, so you don't have to finish everything in one sitting.

Before you finalize your order, it's a good idea to review each page carefully. Make sure photos aren't blurry or cropped in an awkward way, and check any text for spelling mistakes. Most services show you a full preview of your project before you pay, giving you a chance to make final adjustments.

If you're wondering how long it takes to receive your finished book or gift, most companies ship within a week or two, though times can vary during busy holiday seasons. Some even offer expedited shipping if you're in a hurry.

Another benefit of creating photo books and gifts online is that they're easy to duplicate. If you want to give copies of a family reunion book to all your siblings or send identical calendars to each of your children, you can simply order multiples with just a few extra clicks.

9

KEEPING UP THE HABIT

Once you've gotten your photos organized and safely backed up, the next question is: how do you keep up with it? It's a fair question, and one that often gets overlooked until months—or even years—pass and you find yourself back at square one, buried under hundreds of new, unfiled pictures.

Organizing and backing up your photos isn't just a one-time event; it's a habit. The good news is it doesn't have to feel like a burden. Like tending to a garden, a little regular attention keeps things neat, manageable, and enjoyable. And if you establish a routine that works for you, it can actually save you time and frustration in the long run.

The first thing to consider is how often you take pictures. If you're snapping photos every day—grandkids at play, meals you're proud of, garden progress—you'll likely need to sort through them more often than someone who only takes pictures a few times a month. The pace of your photo-taking can guide how often you sit down to tidy things up.

A monthly routine works well for many people. At the end of each month, spend an hour or two reviewing the pictures you've taken during those weeks. This keeps the task small and manageable. It also gives you the chance to delete duplicates, blurry shots, and photos you know you won't want to keep before they pile up.

If you're more of a casual photographer, every three months might be enough. Pick a time that's easy to remember, like the start of each season. This can also make it more enjoyable, as you'll get to relive the memories of that time in your life while you work.

Another approach is to link photo organization to certain events. If you always take pictures during holidays or family gatherings, plan to organize and back them up shortly after those occasions. This way, you stay on top of things and can quickly share the best shots with family while the memories are still fresh.

Whatever frequency you choose, consistency is key. Mark it on your calendar, set a reminder on your phone, or even write it on a sticky note and place it near your computer. Making it part of your routine turns it into a habit you're less likely to skip.

Backing up your photos should happen on a similar schedule, but ideally more often. Technology isn't perfect, and it's better to back up too often than not enough. For many, once a month is a good rhythm. If you take a lot of pictures, once a week might be even better.

Some backup tools can actually handle this automatically. Cloud services often run in the background, quietly saving new pictures every day or whenever your device is connected to Wi-Fi. If you've set up an external hard drive, you can also schedule automatic backups to run at night while you're asleep.

Even if you have automatic backups, it's a good idea to manually check once in a while to make sure everything is working as it should. Open your cloud account or external drive and confirm that your latest photos have been saved properly.

When you're thinking about how often to back up, it helps to think about what you'd lose if your phone or computer stopped working tomorrow. If you've backed up your photos a week ago, you only risk losing one week's worth of memories. If it's been six months, that's a lot more at stake.

Regular organization and backup aren't just about being tidy—they're also about peace of mind. Knowing that your favorite pictures are safe and easy to find takes away a lot of stress. It means you won't have to scroll endlessly looking for a birthday shot when you want to print it or send it to someone. And you'll never have to worry about losing everything to a broken device or a lost phone.

Some people like to use their regular photo session as a time of reflection, too. As you go through your pictures, you might notice patterns in your life—how much your grandkids have grown in a year, how your garden has changed from season to season, the special little moments you might have forgotten otherwise. This can turn what feels like a chore into a meaningful ritual.

If you find yourself overwhelmed by the thought of keeping up with it all, remember you don't have to do everything at once. You can break the task into smaller pieces. Spend fifteen minutes one evening just deleting unwanted pictures. On another day, back up your most recent batch of photos. Then, later in the week, you can create a new album or slideshow.

It can also help to keep a checklist of the steps you usually take when organizing. For example:

- Delete unwanted pictures
- Move favorites into albums
- Back up to the cloud
- Back up to an external drive

Having a simple list to follow makes the process smoother and more reassuring.

Over time, you may even find you start organizing a little bit each time you take pictures. Many people develop the habit of quickly deleting blurry or accidental shots right after taking them. Others move their favorite pictures into an album on their phone the same day. These small habits can make your monthly or seasonal sessions much easier.

Finally, don't forget to share the load. If you live with a partner, spouse, or even have tech-savvy grandkids, involve them in the process. They might enjoy helping you pick the best shots, set up backups, or create albums together.

Tips to make it easy and fun

One of the simplest ways to make it easier on yourself is to break it down into bite-sized steps. You don't need to tackle your entire photo collection in one sitting, especially if it's already quite large. Set a timer for twenty minutes and focus on just one part of your library. Maybe one month's worth of photos, or just your latest holiday. When the timer goes off, you can stop or keep going if you're on a roll. Keeping it short removes the sense of drudgery and helps you avoid burnout.

Having a clear workspace also makes a big difference. Whether you're using a phone, tablet, or computer, make yourself comfortable. Find a quiet corner, pour yourself a cup of tea or coffee, and maybe put on some soft music in the background. If you treat it more like a cozy evening activity than a task to get through, you may even start to look forward to it.

Another way to keep it fun is to bring someone else into

the process. Sit down with a spouse, sibling, or even one of your grandchildren and go through photos together. They can help you decide which ones to keep, tell stories you might not remember, and make the time more social. Children and teenagers in particular often enjoy looking at old family pictures, and it can lead to wonderful conversations about your family's history and traditions.

Technology can actually help you here too. Many phones and computers now offer automatic slideshows or "memories" compilations, where they group your photos by date or theme and play them back with music. Watching one of these can be a great starting point. You can enjoy the highlights right away and then dig deeper into organizing if you're inspired.

One tip that works for many people is to add a little reward to the process. After a successful organizing session, treat yourself to something simple: a walk, a favorite snack, a call to a friend. Tying a pleasant reward to the habit can make it feel more positive over time.

It also helps to create some structure. A checklist of small, repeatable steps can take the guesswork out of organizing and backing up. You might write down: delete blurry or duplicate pictures, move favorites into albums, rename files if needed, back up to the cloud, back up to an external drive. Following the same steps each time builds confidence and keeps you on track.

Don't underestimate the value of labels and notes. Many organizing apps and programs let you tag your photos with names, places, or events. Adding just a few keywords now can save you hours later when you're trying to find that one picture of the family barbecue or your trip to the mountains. This can even turn into a creative exercise, as you come up with witty or heartfelt captions for your favorite pictures.

If you're using a cloud service, take a little time to explore its features. Many services will let you share albums directly with family and friends, and some even allow others to contribute their own pictures to the same album. This can turn a solo project into a collaborative one, as relatives share their perspectives on the same events.

One overlooked tip is to pick themes when organizing. Instead of working through photos strictly by date, you can group them by holidays, vacations, milestones, or even by the people in them. This can feel more meaningful and satisfying, as you see an entire story come together. You might create an album just for birthdays, or one that shows your garden growing over the years.

If you're feeling creative, you can even design little projects as you go. As you organize, pick a few favorite shots and turn them into a calendar, a framed print, or a slideshow to play at your next family gathering. Knowing your efforts will lead to something tangible and enjoyable makes the process more rewarding.

For some people, it also helps to remind themselves that perfection isn't the goal. You don't need every single picture to be in its perfect place before you can start enjoying them. Even just organizing a few favorite albums and backing them up properly is a big step forward. Let yourself feel good about progress, even if you're not "done."

APPENDIX

Glossary

Album

On your phone, computer, or in cloud storage, an *album* is a virtual folder where you can group certain photos together. It might help to think of it like the old photo albums you kept on a shelf, but now it's digital. You can create albums for holidays, people, events, or places to make finding pictures later much easier.

Backup

A *backup* is simply an extra copy of your photos, stored somewhere safe in case something happens to the originals. You can back up your pictures to an external hard drive, a cloud service, or even another computer. The idea is to make sure you never lose your memories because of a device failure or accident.

Cloud

When you hear people talk about "the cloud," they're referring to storage provided over the internet instead of on your physical device. Cloud storage lets you save your photos to secure servers that you can access from any of your devices, anywhere you have an internet connection. Services like Google Photos, iCloud, and Dropbox all use the cloud.

Compression

Compression is a way of making photo files smaller so they take up less space on your device or in the cloud. While this is useful for saving space, heavy compression can reduce the quality of the image. Most photo formats, like JPG, use some level of compression automatically.

Duplicate

A *duplicate* is an exact copy of a photo file. When organizing, you may find that you've accidentally saved the same photo more than once. Part of the organizing process is spotting and deleting duplicates to avoid clutter.

External Hard Drive

An *external hard drive* is a separate device you can plug into your computer or even your tablet to store files, including photos. It's about the size of a book and comes in different storage sizes. It's a great way to back up your photos without using the cloud.

File Name

The *file name* is simply the name your photo is saved under. Many cameras and phones name photos something like "IMG_1234" by default, which doesn't tell you much. Renaming files to include dates, events, or names can make them easier to identify later.

File Size

This refers to how much space a single photo file takes up, usually measured in kilobytes (KB), megabytes (MB), or gigabytes (GB). Larger file sizes usually mean higher quality, but they also take up more room on your device.

Format (File Type)

A photo's *format* refers to the way it's saved. Common formats include:

- **JPG (or JPEG):** The most common photo format, good for everyday pictures.
- **PNG:** Better for photos that include text or graphics, often used online.
- **HEIC:** A newer format used by Apple devices, which saves space but may not work on all older devices.
- **RAW:** Used by professional photographers. Very high quality but takes up a lot of space and usually needs special software to edit.

Metadata

Every photo file includes hidden information called *metadata*. This can include when and where the picture was taken, what camera was used, and even settings like the exposure or lighting. Many photo apps let you view or edit metadata if you want to.

Resolution

Resolution refers to how sharp and detailed your photo is, usually measured in pixels. Higher resolution means more detail but also larger file sizes. Photos taken with modern cameras and phones tend to have very high resolution by default.

Sync

When your devices *sync*, it means they automatically update to match each other. For example, if you take a picture on your phone, and your phone and tablet are synced, the photo will also appear on your tablet. This is a big convenience of using cloud services.

Thumbnail

When you're looking at a grid of pictures in your gallery or on your computer, you're actually seeing *thumbnails*. These are small preview versions of your photos that let you browse quickly without opening each one individually.

Trash/Recycle Bin

When you delete a photo, it doesn't always disappear right away. Many devices move it into a temporary *trash* or *recycle bin*, giving you a chance to restore it if you change your mind. Just remember to empty your trash occasionally to free up space.

Upload and Download

When you *upload* a photo, you're sending it from your device to another place, such as cloud storage or social media. When you *download*, you're saving a photo from the internet or cloud back onto your device.

Wi-Fi vs. Cellular Data

When transferring photos to the cloud or between devices, you might use *Wi-Fi* (your home internet connection) or *cellular data* (from your phone plan). Using Wi-Fi is usually faster and doesn't use up your phone's data allowance.

Zoom

When viewing a photo, *zooming* in allows you to see more detail. Keep in mind that if a photo is low resolution, it can look blurry when you zoom in too far.

Cheat sheets

There's something satisfying about having a clear set of steps you can follow without second-guessing yourself. When it comes to organizing and managing your digital photos, a little direction can take away much of the uncertainty. This chapter offers a series of easy-to-follow cheat sheets for the most common devices and platforms seniors tend to use: iPhone, Android, Windows PC, Mac, and popular cloud services. You can keep this section bookmarked or even jot these down on a card to keep by your computer or phone.

No need to rush through them all at once. Start with the device you use most often, and you'll find it becomes second nature faster than you think.

iPhone (Apple)

To Find Your Photos:

1. Tap the **Photos** app (a multicolored flower icon).
2. You'll see two main tabs at the bottom: *Photos* and *Albums*.
3. In *Photos*, you can scroll through all your pictures in date order.
4. In *Albums*, you can view automatically created albums (like *People* or *Places*), and any you've made yourself.

To Create an Album:

1. In the *Albums* tab, tap the + in the top left corner.
2. Tap *New Album* and name it.

3. Select the photos you want to add by tapping them, then tap *Done*.

To Delete a Photo:

1. Find the photo in *Photos* or *Albums*.

2. Tap the trash can icon and confirm by tapping *Delete Photo*.

3. Photos stay in the *Recently Deleted* album for 30 days in case you change your mind.

To Share a Photo:

1. Open the photo.

2. Tap the square-with-arrow icon (the share button).

3. Choose *Mail*, *Messages*, or *Facebook*, depending on how you'd like to share.

Android Phone

To Find Your Photos:

1. Open the **Google Photos** app (multicolored pinwheel icon).

2. You'll see *Photos*, *Albums*, and *Explore* at the bottom.

3. *Photos* shows everything in date order; *Albums* organizes them into categories.

To Create an Album:

1. Go to the *Albums* tab and tap **New Album.**

2. Name it and select your photos by tapping them.

3. Tap *Add* when finished.

To Delete a Photo:

1. Open the photo.

2. Tap the trash can icon and confirm.

3. Deleted photos stay in the *Trash* folder for 30 days.

To Share a Photo:

1. Open the photo.

2. Tap the share icon (three connected dots or lines).

3. Choose how you'd like to send it.

Windows PC

To Find Your Photos:

1. Open the **Photos** app from the Start menu.

2. All your pictures will display by date.

3. You can also navigate through folders using *File Explorer* (yellow folder icon), often under *Pictures* or *Downloads*.

To Create a Folder:

1. Right-click in the *Pictures* folder and select *New Folder*.

2. Name it whatever you'd like (e.g., "Family 2023").

3. Drag and drop photos into the folder.

To Delete a Photo:

1. Right-click on the photo and select *Delete*.

2. Deleted files go into the *Recycle Bin*, which you can empty when you're ready.

To Share a Photo:

1. Right-click the photo.

2. Select *Share*, then choose *Mail* or another app if installed.

Mac Computer

To Find Your Photos:

1. Open the **Photos** app from the Dock or Applications folder.

2. View all photos in date order or by *Albums* on the left.

To Create an Album:

1. In the Photos app, click *File* > *New Album*.

2. Name the album.

3. Drag photos into it.

To Delete a Photo:

1. Select the photo and press the *Delete* key.
2. Photos move to the *Recently Deleted* album for 30 days.

To Share a Photo:

1. Select the photo and click the *Share* button (box with an arrow).
2. Choose your preferred sharing option.

Google Photos (Cloud Service)

To Access:

1. On your computer, go to photos.google.com.
2. Sign in with your Google account.

To Create an Album:

1. Click + *Create*, then *Album*.

2. Select the photos and give the album a name.

To Delete a Photo:

1. Select the photo.
2. Click the trash can icon.

To Share a Photo or Album:

1. Select what you want to share.
2. Click the *Share* icon and enter an email or copy the link.

iCloud (Cloud Service for Apple Users)

To Access:

1. On your computer, go to icloud.com and sign in.
2. Click on the *Photos* icon.

To Create an Album:

1. Click the + at the top and select *New Album*.
2. Name it and add photos.

To Delete a Photo:

1. Select the photo and click the trash can.

To Share a Photo or Album:

1. Select what you'd like to share.

2. Click the *Share* icon and choose your method.

Resources & helpful links

Manufacturer Help Pages

Many of the devices and apps you're already using have their own help websites. They're kept up-to-date and written specifically for the products you already own. If you're unsure about what version you have, it's usually written on the box your device came in or can be found in the settings menu.

- **Apple Support (iPhone, iPad, Mac, iCloud):**
- support.apple.com
- Apple's guides are clear, and you can search for specific questions, like "how to create albums on iPhone" or "restore photos from iCloud."

- **Google Photos Help:**

- support.google.com/photos
- This is where you can learn about backing up photos to Google, sharing albums, and finding deleted pictures.

- **Microsoft Support (Windows PCs):**
- support.microsoft.com
- Look under the "Photos" or "OneDrive" sections for guidance on organizing and storing photos on your computer.

- **Samsung Support (Android phones & tablets):**
- www.samsung.com/us/support
- If you have a Samsung phone or tablet, this is where you'll find help specific to their photo gallery app and cloud storage options.

Online Communities and Forums

Sometimes you just want to ask a question in plain language and hear from other real people who've dealt with the same thing. These communities are friendly and full of helpful advice.

- **Senior Planet:**
- seniorplanet.org
- This site is designed just for older adults learning technology. They even offer free online classes

about smartphones, computers, and organizing digital photos.

- **Reddit r/photography & r/AskTechnology:**
- reddit.com/r/photography and reddit.com/r/AskTechnology
- These forums have plenty of beginners asking questions about digital photo organization. Don't be shy about posting your own question.

- **Apple Discussions:**
- discussions.apple.com
- Apple users share tips and troubleshoot problems here, especially about photos and iCloud.

Video Tutorials

Watching someone else walk through the steps can make things easier to understand than just reading instructions. These channels on YouTube have helpful videos you can pause and replay as needed.

- **TechBoomers:**
- youtube.com/TechBoomers
- Specializes in beginner-friendly tutorials for seniors.

- **TheHelpfulTechie:**

- youtube.com/TheHelpfulTechie
- A calm, step-by-step style that covers Windows, Android, and cloud storage topics.

- **Apple Support Channel:**
- youtube.com/apple
- For iPhone, iPad, and Mac topics, straight from Apple.

Print and Digital Photo Services

If you'd like to turn your digital photos into physical keepsakes like albums, calendars, or framed prints, these services make it easy to upload and order right from your computer or phone.

- **Shutterfly:**
- shutterfly.com
- Well-known for custom photo books, greeting cards, and gifts.

- **Snapfish:**
- snapfish.com
- Similar to Shutterfly but often with competitive pricing.

- **Walgreens Photo:**
- photo.walgreens.com

- Convenient if you'd rather pick up prints the same day at your local store.

- **Mpix:**
- mpix.com
- Higher-end prints and albums with excellent quality.

Backup Services

Even if you're already backing up photos, it's never a bad idea to have a backup of your backup. Here are a few trusted cloud services you can look into, along with their websites to get started:

- **Google One (Google Photos):**
- one.google.com
- Upgrades your free storage and keeps all photos synced.

- **Dropbox:**
- dropbox.com
- A simple way to store photos and files in the cloud.

- **Amazon Photos:**
- amazon.com/photos

- Free unlimited photo storage if you're already an Amazon Prime member.

- **iCloud:**
- icloud.com
- Best for those already using Apple devices.

Free Tools to Help Detect and Delete Duplicates

Sometimes it feels like your photo collection is twice as big as it should be. These tools can help you find and remove duplicates safely.

- **Duplicate Cleaner Free (Windows):**
- digitalvolcano.co.uk/duplicatecleaner.html

- **Gemini 2 (Mac):**
- macpaw.com/gemini

- **Remo Duplicate Photos Remover (iOS & Android):**
- Available in the App Store and Google Play.

www.ingramcontent.com/pod-product-compliance
Lightning Source LLC
LaVergne TN
LVHW090405210926
848480LV00002B/459